LANGUAGE ACQUISITION in a NUTSHELL

A PRIMER FOR TEACHERS

Bill VanPatten
Russell Simonsen

Graphic Design by Paintbox Creative
Cover illustration: istock.com/Lesia_G

ISBN: 978-1-942544-76-0

1001 North Farifax Street, Suite 200
Alexandria, VA 22314

ACKNOWLEDGEMENTS

Authors and scholars may seem to work alone, and while this may be true as they put fingers to keyboard, behind the scenes may be a myriad of people who deserve thanks in various ways. This is certainly true for us. First, we'd like to thank our friends and families who have always supported us in our academic endeavors. You know who you are. Second, we'd like to thank the many scholars in linguistics and language acquisition whose work over the years influenced us or with whom we've had important conversations about the topics found in this book. We wish we could list them all. Some of them are found in our readings. Others, well, they'll just have to accept here that we appreciate our interactions with them. Third, we thank all the folks at ACTFL who helped to make this book happen. We are especially indebted to Joe Vallina and Meg Malone, who worked with us on all phases of this project from beginning to end. Our very special thanks. Finally, we thank all the teachers who, throughout the years, have asked us questions, raised their hands at presentations and workshops, and otherwise pushed us to be the best we could be as teacher-scholars.

To all my former students. — BVP

In memory of Joan Simonsen — RS

TABLE OF CONTENTS

Prologue vii

Chapter 1. The Object of Acquisition 1

Chapter 2. Ordered Development.. 29

Chapter 3: The Basic Ingredients.. 55

Chapter 4: The Centrality of Implicit Learning 83

Chapter 5: Frequently Asked Questions....................................... 115

Prologue

In this book, we focus on second language and how it is acquired. A natural question a reader might ask is, What does this have to do with teaching, and why read this book?

Let's start with decision-making. Teachers make decisions all the time. They make decisions on which textbook to use or whether or not to use a textbook at all. They make decisions about what activities to use in the classroom and on student assessment. They read standards and guidelines from professional organizations and make determinations about their meanings. How do teachers make these and other decisions?

Our belief is that the best teacher decisions are informed decisions—that is, teachers make decisions based on a variety of sources for which they must be informed, including, but not limited to,

- the age and level of the learner,
- availability of materials,
- technological tools,
- the context in which they teach,
- state and local mandates,
- societal expectations,
- the nature of communication,
- the nature of language, and
- the nature of acquisition.

In our experience, the latter three items (especially the last two) are the ones that many teachers are underprepared for in their decision-making process. Without citing specific names and materials, we've surveyed a number of publications used in teacher preparation courses, as well as professional and regional sites with guidelines, standards, and so on. Surprisingly, the nature of language and language acquisition are the most underrepresented topics in such materials. In fact, in some cases, language and language acquisition are absent altogether. One possible reason is that teachers and teacher educators assume what language is and may use their own experiences to fashion some understanding of the nature of language acquisition. Experience can be useful, but it can also be limiting. Consider the following example: A teacher has completed an undergraduate degree in teacher education in a language (e.g., French). The teacher's only exposure to language has been in textbooks she used as a student of French language. Her only exposure to acquisition has been what she believes she has undergone because of what she was asked to do as a student. These limited exposures mean the teacher arrives at an understanding of language acquisition that looks like the following:

- The language rules and "grammar" presented in language textbooks must be what we acquire and what wind up in our heads.
- Non-children learn languages by studying, memorizing, practicing, and taking tests.

These conclusions may then be reinforced by teacher education curricula because the nature of language and language acquisition are largely absent from the teacher's formal education. In this scenario, language is a subject matter similar to history, math, or science. The teacher only needs general principles of education and learning. This teacher, then, may make decisions without consideration for the nature of language and how language is acquired over time.

The purpose of this book, then, is to put some basic notions about language and language acquisition into teachers' hands so they have additional tools and information with which to make as informed decisions as possible. After all, language teachers are *language* teachers. They aren't history teachers or math teachers. So, one would reasonably expect they'd be as informed as possible about the very focus of their efforts. With that said, do we mean to imply that once teachers read this book they will know what to teach and how to teach it? No. We will touch on this topic again in our final frequently asked question in Chapter 5.

This book is meant to provide a brief introduction to language and language acquisition. Nothing presented in this book is controversial (in our estimation). On topics where there might be some disagreement, however, we point out that possibility and discuss why the disagreement may not be much of a disagreement after all. Our goal is to engage teachers about issues at the heart of what they do. We are not here to tell teachers how to teach or what to teach. We simply want teachers to be as informed as possible as they make decisions about what they do and what they expect of their learners—and perhaps what they expect of themselves.

How to Use This Book

Merriam-Webster defines *primer* as a "small introductory book on a subject." As a primer, this book is not meant for a course on language acquisition. There are lots of thick books out there that cover the "A" to "Z" of language and language acquisition and are more suitable for courses on second language (L2) acquisition. Our goal for this book is different. We understand that teachers are busy, so we purposefully kept this book short and focused on offering the basics. Those basics are culled from our experience in working with teachers over the years in professional development workshops and talks, as well as in courses we've taught that focus on language teaching and the questions that come up in classroom discussion. As such, this book can be used in a number of ways:

- It can be used in teacher preparation courses as a supplement to other books and materials. The book's brevity means it can be slipped in over a period of several weeks.
- It can be used for professional development workshops as background reading or a reference.
- It can be used in book discussion groups led by teachers and local and state supervisors.
- It can be read by any individual on a rainy or snowy weekend.

Overview of This Book

Here are some features in each chapter that you may find useful, as well as the intent behind them:

- *Before You Read:* These boxes are placed at the beginning of the chapter to encourage you to consider some common beliefs and ideas. At the end of the chapter, you are invited to return to them to see if your ideas have changed.
- *Quick Reflection:* These boxes ask you to relate something you've read to experiences you have as a teacher or ideas you have about teaching. Because their purpose is to get you thinking, there are no right or wrong answers, and in some cases the questions may challenge you because you might not have thought about them before.
- *In a Nutshell:* These boxes summarize the main points in the section and invite you to think about the topic a bit more.
- *Selected References and Suggested Readings:* These lists include the work of particular people we quote in the chapter. We also suggest readings so you can cover a topic in more depth should you have the time and inclination.
- *Thinking Some More:* These end-of-chapter questions invite you to ponder some of the main ideas presented in the chapter. In some cases, you are invited to do a little more reading or to interact with others on the topics.
- *Considering the Classroom:* These questions take you a step beyond the Quick Reflections and ask you to consider how certain ideas might influence your own teaching and curriculum development.
- *FAQs:* The frequently asked questions (FAQs) direct you to Chapter 5, where we answer particular questions relevant to the current chapter content.

Chapter 5, "Frequently Asked Questions," is the most flexible part of the book. This chapter is considerably longer than the others due to the 15 questions it addresses. But because each question can stand alone, you do not need to read this chapter all at once. For example, particular FAQs can be read in conjunction with other chapters. We have inserted references to those

FAQs at the end of each chapter that are the most relevant to that chapter's content. This allows you to read a chapter along with FAQs that may address some lingering questions raised by the content of the chapter you have just finished. Or, if you wish, you can wait and read Chapter 5 all by itself, tackling one question at a time when you like.

To the best of our ability, we take a reader-friendly tone in this book. We are academics by training but did not want to write a book for other academics. Those books already exist. We wanted something just for teachers and teachers in training. For this reason, our style is much less academic than what the reader would find in a journal or in one of the big, thick books on language acquisition. Our hope is that the book is easily readable by just about anyone—even non-teachers. If not, please let us know. We encourage interaction between readers and authors!

One last comment about the content of this book: Chapter 1 focuses on the nature of language. Most of the ideas in that chapter can be found in other publications by Bill VanPatten (e.g., *While We're on the Topic* and *The Nature of Language*, both published by ACTFL). If the reader is familiar with those books, Chapter 1 may sound repetitive. However, this book has to stand alone; we can't assume anyone has read about language or language acquisition prior to picking up this book. Thus, it was necessary to include Chapter 1 and focus on the nature of language so that all readers—regardless of their backgrounds—would be on the same page.

About the Authors

We both have formal education in both linguistics and language acquisition, as well as extensive experience with language teaching. As a result, we bring a unique insight to language teaching not often found in "methods" textbooks or other publications that have teachers as their primary audience.

Bill has had a long and distinguished award-winning career in second language research, which includes linking insights from the research on acquisition to language teaching with a focus on communication and proficiency. He has published a number of best-selling college-level language textbooks in Spanish and French, along with readers for beginning- and intermediate-level learners of Spanish. He also hosted the radio shows and podcasts *Tea with BVP* and *Talkin' L2 with BVP*, which aired for almost 5 years combined. Although his principal languages are English, Spanish, and French, Bill has worked with students in researching and discussing other languages, such as German, Japanese, Russian, and Classical Latin. Bill has branched out into fiction, publishing several novels and collections of short stories. To see what he's up to, visit his website (http://www.billvanpatten.net).

Russ is a former high school Spanish teacher who went on to earn a doctorate in Hispanic linguistics with an emphasis on second language acquisition and second language processing. He is a former president of the Minnesota chapter of the American Association of Teachers of Spanish and Portuguese and a current member of the professional development committee for the Ohio Foreign Language Association. For his day job, he is an assistant professor of Spanish at Miami University in Oxford, Ohio, where he teaches courses in linguistics and language acquisition. He also holds a certificate in health care interpretation and is currently working with students to develop an open-access online textbook about health care and the Hispanic community in the United States, *La salud de la comunidad hispana en Estados Unidos*.

Bill and Russ met years ago at a conference in Minneapolis. Bill was a featured speaker and had forgotten his adapter for charging his laptop. A colleague introduced him to Russ, who was a graduate student at the time at the University of Minnesota. Russ graciously offered to take Bill to Best Buy so he could purchase an adapter—and that was the start of a friendship that has deepened and endured. Along the way, they've learned just how much they have in common, other than an interest in linguistics, language acquisition, and language processing. Both are of mixed descent with Latina mothers and non-Latino fathers. Both are singers, although Bill confesses Russ is a much better singer than he is (but maybe he is a better entertainer than Russ). Both are bowlers, even if Russ's height advantage gives his ball toss a little more umph. And the list goes on. After working together on this book, they look forward to a continued friendship and possible other projects down the road.

1

Chapter 1

The Object of Acquisition

Language can be a confusing concept, one that often means different things to different people. To understand language acquisition, we need to understand just what language is.

Before You Read

Consider these statements, then come back after reading this chapter to see if your thoughts have changed.

- I have a working definition of *language* and can state it right now in 50 words or fewer.
- For me, language is communication and communication is language.
- I can verbalize and describe the language that's in my head and tell someone the rules.
- Only humans have language; other animals don't.

It may seem silly to begin a book about language acquisition by asking the question, "What is the object of acquisition?" Or, to put the question another way, "What gets acquired during language acquisition?" The answer may seem obvious: language! But how many of us have a good working definition of *language*? Truth be told, most of us don't have such a definition. We have an *idea* about what it is, we might *think* we know what it is, but most language instructors never take a course on the nature of language and most are never asked to define it. We tend to labor with a vague notion of language—and it's problematic for many of us that this vague notion may be no different from the understanding that non-teachers have, putting teachers' expertise in question. In short, the very thing that is the object of our efforts may elude us in terms of its nature. And for a book like this one, we need to begin with a working definition of *language* so that everyone is on the same page (no pun intended) when we talk about acquisition.

Let's look at what some people have told us language is (you might even find these ideas embedded in definitions on the internet):

- a set of patterns
- a set of rules
- a set of symbols
- a system of communication
- a social system for a community

What these ideas all have in common is that they are, at best, marginally correct. But they are so marginally correct as to not be useable when talking about what language really is. So, let's take a definition derived from the scientific study of language, linguistics. In linguistics, language is an abstract, complex, implicit mental representation of the formal properties of words, sounds, constraints on sentence structure, meaning, and how these relate to each other.

In another ACTFL book, *The Nature of Language*, Bill deals with this definition in detail. We invite you to check out that volume if you want to read about the definition in more depth. In this chapter, we are going to offer just a glimpse of what language is, but this glimpse should be enough to push you toward the notion that perhaps language isn't what we all might think it is.

Language is an abstract, complex, implicit mental representation of the formal properties of words, sounds, constraints on sentence structure, meaning, and how these relate to each other.

Language as Mental Representation

In the previous section, we used the term *mental representation* to introduce what language is. This idea suggests that we don't need to speak or hear for us to have language. American Sign Language is a language, for example, yet the Deaf community in the United States neither hears nor speaks in the everyday sense of these words. But imagine the following: A non-deaf 15-year-old has a skateboard accident and winds up in the hospital. Her head has been injured. She lies there awake but unable to speak. The doctor says, "Tap with one finger for *yes* and tap twice for *no*. Do you understand?" And the teen taps once. Clearly, there is something in this teen's head that allows her to understand the doctor even though she is unable to vocalize anything. That stuff in her head is language. One more example: You, the reader, have just read hundreds of words on this page, organized into several sentences. You didn't speak or hear a thing. But you have something in your head that allows you to make sense of what's on the page. That thing is language.

So, let's turn our attention now to what language is, starting with the idea that, as mental representation, it is abstract.

Abstract

What does *abstract* mean? It's challenging to come up with a definition because, well, like the famous Supreme Court justice's statement about obscenity, you know it when you see it. For our purposes, let's use this statement: Language is abstract because it defies easy explanation or description using everyday terms. The key here is "everyday terms." What we mean is that it's not easy to talk about language in any accurate way without specialized knowledge and terminology, just like it's not easy to talk about quantum mechanics in any real way without specialized knowledge or terminology. The best way to see this challenge is using an example of how we talk about language in ordinary terms and how woefully inadequate these terms are.

As language teachers, we all know what a verb is, right? Let's look at what some people say, then let's see why what they say doesn't work.

"A verb represents an action." This definition works when there are actors who perform actions such as *eat* (*eater*) and *run* (*runner*), but it fails when we have non-actions like *exist* (there's no such thing as an *exister*) and *be* (we don't think we've ever heard of a *be-er*).

"A verb represents a state." This definition works for some states such as *exist, have,* and *love,* but then consider all the states that aren't verbs: *happy, bothered,* and *messed up*. That is, adjectives can represent states. So, states can't necessarily be equated with verbs.

"A verb is the central part of a sentence." Just what does it mean for something to be central? In the sentence "Bill is not tall," is Bill the central part because the sentence is about him? Is *not tall* the central part because that's the comment we're making? Is the meaningless verb *is* central? To be sure, we can express complete ideas without verbs, as in "So?" and "Big deal." Plus, there are languages in which certain kinds of verbs aren't required (e.g., in Mandarin, to say "Bill is not tall," you would just say *Bǐ'ěr bù gāo* 'Bill not tall'). In addition, we have auxiliary verbs and so-called linking verbs, which carry no meaning, so they can't be central (e.g., *do* as in "Do you like almond milk?").

"A verb carries the tense of the sentence." This is true for English but not for Mandarin or Vietnamese, for example—languages that don't put tense on verbs. So, verbs don't work the same in all languages.

"A verb agrees with the subject." First, we have to define *subject*, and that's another problem. You are defining an abstract concept with an equally abstract concept. Second, verbs don't always agree with subjects. English has virtually no agreement (e.g., "I/you/the dog/we/you can" and "Bob, Bill, and Meg ate" and only "s" is added to third-person singular in the present), Chinese and Japanese have no agreement with verbs at all, and some languages have "spotty" agreement in that agreement is not consistent (e.g., French uses the sound sequence */parl/* for first-, second-, and third-person singular as well as third-person plural, while only first- and second-person plural sound different [*/parlõ/* and */parle/*, respectively]). Only languages like Spanish and Russian have what is called *rich agreement*, where the verb generally has to agree with the subject for almost every single person and number combination.

By now, the point is clear. We all "know" what a verb is, yet we have difficulty pinpointing its nature. We simply know one when we see one. Constructs such as verbs, nouns, subjects, and others in language are abstract concepts that defy accurate descriptions or definitions

Constructs such as verbs, nouns, subjects, and others in language are abstract concepts that defy description in everyday terms.

in everyday terms. They exist in our heads, but we can't quite say what they are without being inaccurate, roundabout, reliant on other equally abstract ideas, or all of these things combined.

Quick Reflection

A student in class asks you, "What's a verb?" What would you say?

Let's take a second example: what many people would call a "rule." Language consists of rules, right? Here's one.

Use *I* as a subject and *me* as an object (of a verb or preposition).
Example: "I went to the store," not "*Me went to the store."
Example: "The teacher called me," not "*The teacher called I."

This looks like a rule, and most of us know this one. But what's really in our heads, and how do subject pronouns and object (non-subject) pronouns work? Can you, the reader, explain why we hear the follow sentences all the time (except for those marked with an asterisk, as is done throughout the book)? The fact that they are said makes them possible in English, despite what your grammar school teacher told you—that is, we're not talking about "bad English" here. We're talking about something in the English speaker's mind that allows and disallows certain kinds of sentences.

(1) John and I went to the store.
(2) John and me went to the store.
(3) Me and John went to the store.

(4) They told it to Murphy and me at the same time.
(5) They told it to Murphy and I at the same time.
(6) *They told it to I and Murphy at the same time.

(7) Who's in? Me.
(8) Who's in? *I.
(9) Who's in? *Me am.
(10) Who's in? I am.

It looks like our rule for subjects versus objects doesn't work so well. Something much more abstract about when *I* and *me* are permissible is at work in our heads. Interestingly, in French, with compound noun subjects, *je* (*I*) is prohibited: *Jean et moi sommes allés au resto* 'John and I/me went to the restaurant.' **Jean et je sommes allés* is not allowed. Also disallowed is *me* 'me': **Jean et me sommes allés*. And a language like Spanish disallows anything other than a subject pronoun in compound noun subjects: *Juan y yo fuimos al restaurante/*Juan y me fuimos al restaurante*. So, what is allowed or required in one language may not be the same for another. In short, subject pronouns don't always behave the same way in different languages. Subjects and their pronouns have abstract properties that cause them to behave in certain ways under certain conditions.

Here's another example of something that's abstract, but maybe just a little less so. Textbooks erroneously call such things as *my* and *your* possessive adjectives. While they do indicate possessors, they are not adjectives, strictly speaking. Why do we call them possessive adjectives? And if they aren't possessive adjectives, what are they? Let's look at these sentences:

(11) That's my house.
(12) That's the house.
(13) That's the red house.
(14) *That's the my house.

In looking at these sentences, we see *the* (often called a definite article) and *red* (a descriptive adjective denoting color). The two can combine to form "the red house." But if *my* is an adjective, why can't it combine with *the* to form "the my house"? It can't be combined for this purpose because *my* is not an adjective, but rather is the same class of grammatical device as *the*. Linguists call words such as *my* and *the* determiners. "The my house" is ungrammatical because English doesn't normally allow two determiners back to back in a sentence. This is true in other languages as well (Spanish: **la mi casa*; French: **la ma maison*; German: **der mein Haus*). In Italian, *la mia casa* is possible, but in this case, *mia* is actually an adjective. It originates after the noun, then gets moved to another spot in the sentence (*la casa mia* → *la mia casa).* In fact, something like *Casa mia è dietro l'angolo* 'My house is around the corner' is common in spoken Italian. So, those of you who speak Italian shouldn't think that Italian violates what we just said about two determiners back to back: Something like *mia* really is an adjective.

Now, with all of that said, here is the question: What's a determiner? If you google this word, you'll come up with inadequate definitions. For linguists, a determiner is a functional element that occupies a particular spot in a sentence. Here are some determiners: *some/any, each,* and *this/these.* Try the test above with *the* and see what happens (e.g., "*The some people are here," "*The each dog has a toy"). The concept of a determiner defies easy definition in everyday language.

We'll stop here. There's plenty written elsewhere about the abstract nature of language. As we said earlier in this chapter, the book *The Nature of Language* can help you explore more about the abstract nature of language and really get a feel for this topic. We also provide additional readings at the end of this chapter. For now, we'll just say the following: What's on textbook pages isn't what winds up in anyone's head. Such rules aren't psychologically real. In other words, language is more abstract than the "concrete" rules and patterns presented in textbooks. In fact, what textbooks try to do is what we all try to do if we aren't practicing linguists: They try to describe for students the indescribable—and because of these efforts, they generally get things wrong.

In a Nutshell ...

Language isn't rules or charts. There's no list somewhere that says, "This is what English is" or "This is what Chinese is." Every learner of a language must build an abstract representation of the language being learned over time—and that representation can't be found in textbooks.

Try this exercise with your friends: Ask them to tell you why the sentences with asterisks are not possible in English. (That is, can they tell you when it's possible to contract in English and when it's not?)

1. I've done it/*Should I've done it?
2. I'm going to eat/I'm gonna eat/I'm going to the store/*I'm gonna the store.
3. Who do you want to invite?/Who do you wanna invite?/*Who do you wanna send out the invitations?
4. Harriet is English and Jane is, too/Harriet's English and Jane is, too/*Harriet's English and Jane's, too.

Quick Reflection

If textbooks typically provide ideas about language that are inadequate or wrong, do you think teachers need better rules and explanations in textbooks?

Complex

Any dictionary definition of *complex* goes something like this: "composed of multiple parts." This definition seems straightforward, right? But let's not forget that these multiple parts have to interact in certain ways. Think of something as complex as an airline company. For that company to function, what components have to work together? We can list some components (the tip of the iceberg):

- pilots
- flight attendants
- clerks at check-in
- clerks at the gate
- mechanics
- baggage people
- TSA crew
- air traffic controllers
- the baggage conveyor system
- chefs
- cleaning crews
- loading crews
- software systems
- hardware
- food trucks
- fuel trucks

For every flight we take, dozens of different components interact so that flight can take off. What happens when we apply the notion of complexity to language? We can use any given simple sentence to illustrate complexity. Let's break down the complexity of this one: "There's a fly in my soup."

Lexicon refers to words. Each of us has a mental dictionary in which we store words. Most of us think we just store meaning so that *soup* refers to a liquid dish normally served in a bowl. But also encoded along with that meaning are certain grammatical properties required for that word to participate in a sentence. In this case, the word is marked with "N" to indicate that it's a noun. It's also tagged as both *mass* and *count*, which means that in the singular it can co-occur with both *some* ("I bought some soup") and *the/a* ("I bought the soup"). Compare this example with a noun such as *herd*, which can only be a count noun in the singular (e.g., "I saw a herd of buffalo" but not "*I saw some herd of buffalo"). Words are "inserted" into sentences, but they can't just be inserted anywhere. There is a complex interaction between their meanings (if they have any), their grammatical properties, and other components of language.

Syntax refers to constraints on sentence structure. For example, English requires overt subjects when there is a verb in the sentence. The answer to the question "Where's Russ?" can only be "He's at the office," not "*Is at the office." The subject pronoun *he* is required. Because English generally requires overt subjects in simple sentences, we rely on what are called expletive subjects such as *there* and *it*. "There's a fly in my soup" is possible in English, but "*Is a fly in my soup" is not. As another example, "It's raining" is possible in English, but "*Is raining" is not. If you speak Spanish, you know that the opposite is true: Spanish does not have expletive subjects, and subjectless sentences are not only possible but required under certain conditions, such as in the two examples we just saw: *Hay una mosca en mi sopa* and *Está lloviendo*. As another example, languages have what is called phrase structure (e.g., noun phrases, verb phrases, prepositional phrases). English is a language with underlying phrases that follow what is called head-complement order. Thus, the prepositional phrase "in my soup" consists of the head *in* plus its complement *my soup*. The phrase *my soup* has a particular order because it's a determiner phrase and the determiner *my* heads the phrase and the complement *soup* follows. The opposite is true for Japanese, which is complement-head, as in "soup my in." In this one little sentence, "There's a fly in my soup," there are at least a half dozen hidden constraints all happening at once to make this sentence look the way it does.

Morphology refers to the shapes of words. So, as one example, *soup* and *soups* are different because one has a plural marker and one doesn't. This represents how plurality in English is normally reflected in a *morphological inflection* on nouns. Note that the minute we make our sentence about more than one fly, a number of things change (e.g., verb form, noun endings): "There are flies in our soups." To be sure, in spoken English, we often say and hear "There's flies in here." That sounds fine, but "There's flies in our soups" sounds a bit less "good" to some people (but still permissible). Then there's the following, which is just not permissible: "*There are a fly in my soup."

Quick Reflection

Does your language have verb endings to indicate person and number (i.e., who the subject is)? How concerned are you that learners have to "master" such endings or are you patient that they will eventually "get it"?

Phonology refers to the underlying properties of sounds, while *phonetics* refers to how these sounds are pronounced during real-time speech. For example, the phonological representation of a plural marker in English is /s/. But the actual sound is not always [s]. It can be [s], [z], or [ɪz]. Here are samples: *book/books* [s], *fly/flies* [z], *house/houses* [ɪz]. What is more, phonology and phonetics are implicated in how we handle things like contractions, syllable structure, what happens at word boundaries, and so on. Note that in our sentence, "There's a fly in my soup," when we speak this sentence, we normally move the [z] sound of *there's* to the next word (*a*), as in "There zuh fly in my soup." But we can only do this because the next word begins with a vowel. If it began with a consonant, we couldn't do it: "There's fresh coffee" = "Therez fresh coffee." How sounds work with each other in syllable formation adds another layer of complexity to a sentence.

Prosody refers to the rhythm and pitch of a sentence. Normally this is reflected in where weak and strong stresses are found and where our tone rises or falls. In a normal declarative statement for "There's a fly in my soup," the strongest stress would be on *fly:* "There's a FLY in my soup." As a speaker's intent to convey something particular changes, the stress and pitch may change. For example, "There's a fly in MY soup (not your soup)" or "There's a fly in my SOUP (not on the table)."

Meaning in language has at least two components. One is literal meaning. A person can make an observation and simply say, "There's a fly in my soup." But that person can also say this in a certain way to indicate a second meaning, which is his or her intent. Maybe that person wants to complain or show disgust. That person would then say the sentence a different way (and maybe do other things, too, such as make a face). Almost every sentence has at least two layers of meaning: literal and speaker intent.

The point is that for every single sentence, there is a complex interplay between the lexicon, syntax, morphology, phonology, phonetics, prosody, and meaning. These components enter into a coordinated dance that can boggle the mind the more closely we inspect what is happening. And we're just touching the tip of the iceberg here, and with a very simple sentence as an example. The takeaway is that for any given sentence, no matter how simple, no matter its length, there is a complex interaction of components that are all required to work at lightning speed for that sentence to exist. How is this complexity ever acquired? And note that the complexity increases when we deal with multiple sentences and clauses that work together in conversation or text.

For every single sentence, there is a complex interplay between the lexicon, syntax, morphology, phonology, phonetics, prosody, and meaning.

In a Nutshell ...

Every sentence is composed of a complex interplay between different parts of language (e.g., the sound system, syntactic operations, words, word forms, pitch and tone, meaning). All of the parts work together in a way such that just the removal of one might throw off the sentence or even render it uninterpretable. We used the analogy of an airline company to get into this topic. Can you think of other systems that are also complex?

How would you say, "There's a fly in my soup" in the language you teach? Can you deconstruct the sentence to see how complex it is?

Implicit

In everyday language, the term *implicit* refers to something unsaid and is related to the verb *imply*. But in language, we use *implicit* to mean *unconscious*. That is, we are unaware of the nature of language in our heads. We know we have it; we are conscious of that. However, we are not conscious of its contents—and when we try to articulate its contents, we generally run into trouble.

We can return to an example from one of the previous sections to illustrate what we mean. Do you remember our discussion of what a verb is? We had difficulty with saying just what constitutes a verb, yet we all have knowledge of verbs and "know one when we see one." That knowledge is implicit. For years, we've been using language without giving a thought to what a verb really is. In short, we have implicit knowledge about what makes a verb a verb, a noun a noun, a preposition a preposition, and so on.

In linguistics, we often demonstrate implicit knowledge by demonstrating both what we know is possible in a language and what is impossible, even though we can't say why. Here's an example we like to use: We can use *re-* as a prefix with verbs to mean "do again," as in *decorate/redecorate*, *do/redo*, and *read/reread*. But what about the following sentences?

> We often demonstrate implicit knowledge by demonstrating both what we know is possible in a language and what is impossible, even though we can't say why.

(15) She pet the dog and when it wagged its tail, she repet it.

(16) I stepped in the puddle and then restepped in it.

(17) I was tired when I woke up so I reslept a little.

You probably bristled at the use of *re-* with the verbs *pet*, *step*, and *sleep*. Why? What's the "rule" for using *re-* with verbs? Our dollar bet is that you can't really say why, yet you know possible and impossible uses of *re-* when confronted with them. You also have implicit knowledge about which verbs that begin with *re-* actually have a prefix and which have *re-* as part of the root: *redo* and *recount* versus *record* and *reveal*. But that's another issue. In short, you have implicit knowledge of how *re-* works with verbs, but it is almost impossible for you to say what that knowledge is.

Quick Reflection

How much concern do you put on the idea that learners develop an implicit system (i.e., a system they are unaware of)?

Here's one more example to illustrate what we mean by implicit knowledge along with what is possible and impossible. This example comes from the sound system, what linguists call *phonology*. There is such a thing as devoicing of consonants. *Voicing* refers to whether or not the vocal cords vibrate when you're producing a consonant. You can check this out by gently placing two fingers on your vocal cord area and pronouncing these two sounds: [s] as in *sue* and [z] as in *zoo*. With the [z], you should feel the vibration in your throat, but you won't feel it when producing [s]. The [z] is voiced and the [s] is not.

In English, you can devoice consonants at the end of a word. Not everyone does it, but it's possible. This is why some people say *Japanese* with a [z] sound at the end and some people say the same word with an [s] at the end. But note two things. First, you can only do this with certain words. You would never devoice *these*, for instance. It's always pronounced with a [z] sound. And the opposite never happens. You never voice something that is normally not voiced. So, you never say *police* with a [z] at the end; it always has an [s]. Second, devoicing never happens in word-initial position. For example, *zebra* and *zany* are always pronounced with a [z] and never an [s]. What are the rules for devoicing then? And why can't you voice consonants that are normally not voiced? People have implicit knowledge about how the sound system works, just like they have implicit knowledge about everything else in language.

To be sure, people "get" conscious knowledge about language during formal education. But most of this conscious knowledge is about prescriptive matters that have nothing to do with how language really works. For example, "don't end a sentence in a preposition" is a grammatical rule that many English speakers are taught. And if we return to an earlier example, people are explicitly taught that they shouldn't say "me and John" and should say "John and I." Yet our implicit system allows for both prepositions at ends of sentences (e.g., "That's the man I talked to") and "me and John" as the subject of a sentence; in fact, both are the norm in spoken language. People are taught not to use *ain't*, that it's "bad language" or "bad grammar," yet we use it all the time. And we have implicit knowledge about how to use it: "I ain't got none" is possible, but "*I ain't have any" sounds awful.

So, we're not talking about the "rules of grammar" and "proper language" we are taught in school or in writing classes. We're talking about what actually exists in our heads and what is possible or impossible in terms of representation. All of this representation of language is implicit. It is unconscious and largely unavailable for easy description with everyday words and ideas.

In a Nutshell ...

We carry around a linguistic system in our heads, the content of which is largely inaccessible to us. This is as true in a second and subsequent language as it is in a first language, which is why mental representation for language is implicit. We know it's there, but we have difficulty saying exactly *what* is there.

Are there other things we know that are implicit? Things that aren't language? Things that we know them when we see them, but we can't quite define what they are in everyday simple language?

Interim Summary

So language is (a) mental representation that is (b) abstract, (c) complex, and (d) implicit in nature. It is a fascinating aspect of human knowledge and ability—and one of the aspects of our lives that we take for granted. The common college-educated person knows more about evolution, how the human eye works, and how weather systems form than he or she knows about what language is. To be sure, language is not what we find in textbooks. It's just too abstract and complex to be put into neat little rules on the page of a Level 1 textbook or an eighth-grade grammar lesson.

You might be asking yourself, "Do all linguists agree with the picture painted here?" We are trained in theoretical linguistics and psycholinguistics and have a particular framework we use to talk about language that is called *generative*. Not all linguists are generativists, and they may not agree with the framework. However, linguists do agree with the general thesis here: Language is abstract, complex, and implicit and is not what we find in language textbooks. How about psychologists? Most psychologists working in language acquisition don't adhere to a specific definition of language, although recently some of these psychologists have begun to look at an alternative to generative approaches to language. This alternative is called *construction grammar*, developed by linguists who do not agree with the basic generative perspective on the nature of language. However, psychologists working in language acquisition would agree that language is abstract, complex, implicit, and not digestible on the pages of language textbooks. We will touch on these ideas now and then in this book.

Language and Communication

A potential problem in talking about language is that many people confuse it with communication. Let's look at the first sentence in a Wikipedia entry we found: "A language is a structured system of communication." This is a misleading way to begin a description of language, and we'll see why as we progress in this section. We'd like to correct this entry and get the ball rolling by saying the following: Language can form a part of communication, but it is not equivalent to communication.

So, let's talk about communication. Our favorite definition of communication (and the most widely accepted definition in applied linguistics circles) is this: "Communication is the expression and interpretation of meaning in a given context for a given purpose." Central to this definition are the constructs of meaning, context, and purpose. We touched on meaning earlier when we examined the simple sentence "There's a fly in my soup." We saw that there are at least two levels of meaning in this sentence: the literal meaning and what the speaker wants the listener to grasp about the intent of this sentence. For example, if a server hears this sentence from a customer, she might interpret it to mean the customer wants a new soup. So, someone is expressing meaning and someone is interpreting that meaning. There's not a lot more to say about this except the following: If communication is dependent on meaning, and if language is the same as communication, wouldn't all aspects of language be meaning related? We know this is clearly false. Let us offer some quick examples.

Earlier, we said that English requires expletive subjects such as *there* and *it*, such as in "There's a fly in my soup" (not "*Is a fly in my soup"). Yet languages such as Spanish don't have expletives, and in fact the only way to say this sentence is something similar to the ungrammatical sentence in English. What purpose for *meaning* do expletive subjects have if some languages don't have them? What does *there* contribute to the meaning that an insect is floating in someone's meal?

Here's a second example. We also touched on word order earlier when we said that English is head-complement and Japanese is complement-head in talking about how phrases are constructed (e.g., noun phrases, verb phrases, prepositional phrases). The head-complement nature of English causes the following phrases, with the heads of the phrase in capital letters:

- THERE + is a fly in my soup
- IS + a fly in my soup
- A + fly in my soup
- IN + my soup
- MY + soup

Japanese is complement-head, and its underlying phrase structure is different. With apologies for taking shortcuts to illustrate here, the "fly sentence" would have this kind of word order:

- watashi no sūpu ni hae ga IMASU 'my soup in fly + IS'
- watashi no sūpu NI 'soup my + IN'
- watashi NO 'MY' (Note that *my* in Japanese would be a compound head-final phrase consisting of the particle *no* [= possessing] attached to the possessor—that is, *watashi* 'I'; the particle *no* is the head of the possessive phrase)

Why do languages have different underlying word orders to express the same meaning? What does head-complement versus complement-head have to do with making meaning? It doesn't have anything to do with meaning, actually. So always tying language into meaning-making can be a problem if we really want to understand what language is.

Why do languages have different underlying word orders to express the same meaning? Always tying language into meaning-making can be a problem if we really want to understand what language is.

Grammatical gender is another example of a meaningless linguistic device. Many languages have grammatical gender or, better yet, classes of nouns. Spanish and French have two, German has three, and Swahili has nine. It's unfortunate we refer to them as gender because outside of animate nouns, there is no gender for concepts like paper, rock, and scissors. Languages that have noun classes also have agreement so that adjectives, determiners, and other elements have to match in some way. What meaning is there to, for example, have a *maison* 'house' in French be *la maison* as opposed to **le maison* or in German *das Haus* instead of **die/*der Haus*?

The next point we want to make is this: Context affects communication, but it doesn't affect language. Context refers to participants and setting—in other words, *social* context. These two constructs interact to push us to communicate differently under different conditions. Let's go back to our sample sentence with *fly*. Which of these sentences is more likely to be said to a close friend, and which is more likely to be said to a server in a restaurant who the client does not know personally?

- Excuse me. There's a fly in my soup. [nice, neutral voice]
- I'm gonna vomit! There's a fly in my soup! [excited tone, pitch rises]

If you are a typical communicator in English, you'd say the second one could only be used with a close friend and not the server. Why? Because the two contexts are different. We talk to close friends differently than how we talk to servers we don't know—and of course the setting can make a difference. We'd say, "I'm gonna vomit!" in situations where it is acceptable (e.g., when we're alone, when we're with friends, when we text friends). And we'd be more likely to say, "Excuse me" in a nice restaurant as we call over the server. But here's the point we want to make: Regardless of the context, the structure of the sentence doesn't change. We still have to use an expletive subject. We don't switch from "There's a fly in my soup" to "*Is a fly in my soup" depending on whether we're talking to a server or to a friend or we're in a dive bar or a four-star restaurant. And the verb doesn't change from *is* to *are* depending on who we're talking to (e.g., "*There are a fly in my soup"). And of course we don't suddenly switch to Japanese-like word order and cry out, "Fly soup my in is!" Why? Because language doesn't change depending on con-

Language doesn't change depending on context. What changes is what we select from language to express meaning.

text. Language can only do certain things. What changes is what we select from language to express meaning.

Our last construct within communication that we will touch on is purpose. When we communicate, we always have some reason for doing so. We want to be social, make friends, get a job done, find something out or inform someone of something, entertain someone or some group of people. As we write this section, our purpose is to inform the reader about the difference between language and communication. The reader moves along the page hoping to find something out, gain insight into something. We have a purpose here during the communicative act of writing and reading. But as in the case of context, we can only do certain things with English. We can't make it be something it isn't. We have to put subjects in sentences, we have to use head-complement word order, and so on. Language doesn't change, but how we use it to express meaning might. Here's an example. At this point, we could say, "Do you see how communication and language are not the same thing?" or we could say, "By now, you should have a feel for how communication and language are not the same thing." These are stylistic choices based on how we want to "sound," whether or not we want to invite you to reflect, and maybe simply based on what we've done before (e.g., "Let's see. We asked the reader a question in the last paragraph, so let's not use that device here again"). At the same time, no matter which one we select, the verb has to be *are* and not *is* (e.g., "*Communication and language is not the same thing") and the word *how* can appear in one and only one place in either sentence. This is because language doesn't change depending on purpose; language is mental stuff we draw on during communication, but that mental stuff includes constraints on sentence structure, word structure, sound structure, prosody, and so on.

Quick Reflection

Do you see yourself as a language teacher? Or a teacher of communication using another language? What is the difference between the two?

Before moving on, let's not confuse playing with language and inventing new things with language as indicative of changing language for communication. I can, for example, invent a new verb based on a noun. This is what happened with Google. We now have *Google* as a proper noun denoting a search engine on the internet, but we also have the verb *google*, which means to conduct a search. English is good at making verbs out of nouns. But note that once we make *Google* into *google*, both words have to adhere to all constraints for either names (proper nouns) or verbs. So, you could say, "Bill googled the recipe last night" but not "*Bill will google the recipe last night," or say, "I prefer Google to Yahoo," not "*I prefer the Google to the Yahoo."

We want to address just one more thing before we close out this chapter, and that is the relationship between communication and language. Communication can make use of language. As "mental stuff," language exists in your head regardless of whether you are communicating or not. When you are asleep and not dreaming, language doesn't go away, but communication does. This is why we say language is all in your head.

When we are awake and want to communicate something, we can tap this mental stuff, but we don't have to. If someone asks you where the tea is, you can say, "It's in the pantry," or you can point over your shoulder with your thumb at the pantry. If you're talking to someone and say, "Why are you looking at me like that?" you ask the question because the person has communicated some kind of meaning via a facial expression (e.g., scrunched face, frown, narrowed eyes). No language was used by the other person. And if you've ever learned how to drive, you can tell a stop sign a block away, even if you can't read the word *stop*. The shape and color of the sign communicate something. Finally, it goes without saying that animals communicate with humans in all kinds of ways without language (e.g., tail wagging, growling, purring, bearing teeth). Yet language is a powerful tool for communication, as all the words and sentences on this page suggest.

We will conclude this section about the difference between language and communication by reinforcing the following two points. First, communication is a social act. It is a social act because it takes place between multiple entities in a particular setting (context). There are agreed upon norms about how communication happens socially (e.g., "Say please and thank you";

"Don't yell in public"; and "It's rude to point"). Communication involves doing.

The second point is that language is not about doing but about knowing—and this knowing involves knowing both what is possible and not possible. We know that *remake* is possible but not **redesire*. We know that saying "I've gone" is possible but "*Should I've gone?" is not. We know that "Have you got any money?" "Yes, I have some" is possible, but "Have you got some money? *Yes, I have any" is not. And so on. In short, we have more in our heads than what tumbles out of our mouths and what we've ever heard (or signed and seen). When we communicate, we communicate with only possible sentences in a language, yet we wind up with knowledge about what is not possible. And we also know what is possible even when we've never encountered it, and we know what is impossible without being taught. Social context governs how we use language to communicate, but it doesn't govern the underlying mental representation we have for language.

In a Nutshell ...

Although communication and language may be related, they are not the same thing. Language is something that exists in our heads, while communication is something that occurs in contexts between two or more people or entities. Communication generally (but not always) makes use of language, but even when we don't communicate, language sits there in our heads. It doesn't disappear.

This delineation is important in language teaching, but what about the layperson? Ask around and see what non–language people think language and communication are. What do they say?

We would like to offer one final note about a difference between language and communication. Communication can and does make use of what we might call *chunked language* or *formulas*. Chunks and formulas are phrases and utterances stored as whole units in the lexicon. In English, we use formulas all the time in everyday speech: "Howzit going?" "What's up?" "I dunno," and "Nice to meet you" are examples. Chunks include phrases that aren't complete units into which other things can be inserted. "Pass the ____, please" and "I don't know _____" are two examples. All languages have chunks and formulas that speakers store in their lexicons as whole units (e.g., Spanish *¿Cómo se dice ____?* 'How do you say ___?' and French *Ça va* 'How are things?/Everything good?'). They draw on these in everyday communication—and sometimes in writing—to express meaning. But we also know that communication can't consist only of chunks and formulas. If it did, we could not generate entirely new sentences or understand things we've never heard before. Again, the underlying mental representation of language gives power to communication it might not have otherwise.

Language and Culture

We often hear among professionals that culture is important to the teaching of language. We would certainly agree that culture is important when learning about other people, and before we continue, we want to stress that we do not advocate abandoning teaching about culture in classrooms. But recommendations about the teaching of culture do not fall under the purview of research on the acquisition of language as defined here. We would disagree with any idea that you need to learn about culture to acquire language or that you need to learn language through culture. Why would we make such a bold statement?

First, culture is an elusive concept. While we are able to define and talk about language and communication in this chapter, we are hard pressed to find a good working definition of culture for teachers. (Try a Google search and see what happens.) Culture may include everything from religious and cultural beliefs to rules about polite behavior to the value we place on pets. And even within a culture, there may be cultures and subcultures. The United States, for example, is not a monolithic cultural entity, and those of us who work with Spanish know that there is no such thing as "Hispanic culture." If we can't pinpoint culture, how could we "teach language through culture"? What is more, cultural knowledge seems to be best acquired in context. It is difficult to imagine a classroom in the middle of Iowa that can mimic or incorporate a cultural experience that is, say, Korean or Turkish. One acquires Korean cultural knowledge best by living in Korea.

Second, language as mental representation is not determined by culture, nor is culture determined by language. Let's take an example from earlier in the chapter. Japanese is a complement + head language (e.g., *sūpu* NI 'soup in' and not **NI sūpu* 'in the soup'). On the other side of world, Quechua (spoken by indigenous peoples of the Andes) is also a complement + head language. And 2,000 years ago, Classical Latin was a complement + head language. We can't think of three "cultures" that could be more distinct from each other—and separated by both time and space, yet all three languages share the same basic sentence structure. What does complement + head structure have to do with "being Japanese," "being Roman," or "being Quechua"?

Let's take another example from earlier. We saw that, in English, the plural /s/ sound on nouns can be pronounced as [s], [z], or [Iz] (e.g., book[s], mouth[z], watch[Iz]). Is this a cultural artifact? What does culture have to do with how sounds behave in situations like plural markers in English? The fact of the matter is that culture is not implicated at all in the mental representation we call language—except perhaps in some of the meaning behind certain words and formulas.

We think the idea of teaching culture to learn language is rooted in the confusion we noted in a previous section in this chapter. Many people think language and communication are the same, but they are not. Language is mental representation. It consists of structure, abstract features, and a variety of components that interact to make even the simplest of sentences. Communication is a behavior that happens between people and other entities. It is shaped by social context and manifests itself in different ways depending on who is communicating with whom and for what purpose. How we communicate may be inextricably tied up with culture (again, whatever that is). But language as mental representation is not.

In addition, perhaps without realizing, advocates of teaching language through culture might reduce language to meaning only, especially when it comes to words and ideas. For example, they might point out that what *sensei* really means in Japanese is not exactly the same as *teacher* in American English (and vice versa) and that this difference in meaning is rooted in culture. This observation is not without merit, but we cannot reduce the entirety of language—especially the formal system as described in this chapter—to words and what they mean. In the case of *sensei*, it is not clear that classroom learners in the United States would ever acquire what the word means in all of its senses. It is by living in Japan that a learner appropriates this nuanced cultural knowledge and comes to know how it interacts with meaning.

So, as linguists, we would rephrase what is often said in language teaching circles: We can't teach language through culture. Instead, we learn about culture as we interact and communicate with others from another culture. To the extent that communication makes use of language, then language is part of the tools people use to acquire cultural knowledge as they engage in communication, not the other way around. Individual instructors may choose to place a heavy emphasis on the development of cultural knowledge, especially if it is relevant to students' interests or there is some social, political, or other need to do so. But we caution against the position that the formal properties of language are learned through culture.

Summary

In this chapter, we have reviewed three aspects that are at the core of the nature of language:

- It is abstract.
- It is complex.
- It is implicit.

We've also distinguished between communication and language, showing that they aren't the same thing. Communication is a social act that can make use of language, but language is something that resides in our heads regardless of whether we communicate or not. Communication is dependent on meaning making and the roles of context and purpose, while none of these constructs impact the nature of language itself. That is, if an English-speaking person is in a doctor's office one moment, in a grocery store an hour later, and then at home with a spouse, the English inside that person's head does not change because the context of communication has changed. The subject of a sentence is the subject of a sentence regardless of meaning, context (participants and setting), and purpose (why people engage in communication). A verb is a verb no matter what, and **redesire* is not a possible verb regardless of meaning, context, and purpose (i.e., the ungrammatical nature of **redesire* remains whether we're in a doctor's office, the grocery store, or somewhere else).

As we consider the nature of language acquisition, we are, in essence, asking how this abstract, complex, and implicit representation gets in our heads. Although communication may be an important social act, language is only one of its tools. The acquisition of that tool is fundamental to any way in which communication can make use of language.

Selected References and Suggested Readings

Here are three books by Bill:

VanPatten, B. (2016). *Communication and skill.* Routledge.

VanPatten, B. (2016). *Language.* Routledge.

VanPatten, B. (2019). *The nature of language: A short guide to what's in our heads.* ACTFL.

We also recommend just about any introductory book on linguistics, including the following:

Akmajian, A., Farmer, A. K., Bickmore, L., Demers, R.A., & Harnish, R. M. (2017). *Linguistics: An introduction to language and communication.* MIT Press.

Denham, K., & Lobeck, A. (2013). *Linguistics for everyone.* Cengage Learning.

Fasold, R. W., & Connor-Linton, J. (Eds.). (2014). *An introduction to language and linguistics.* Cambridge University Press.

Fromkin, V., Rodman, R., & Hyams, N. (2007). *An introduction to language* (8th ed.). Thomson-Wadsworth.

Here are some additional books that are classics related to communication:

Murphy, K. (2020). *You're not listening: What you're missing and why it matters.* Celadon Books.

Savignon, S. (1997). *Communicative competence: Theory and classroom practice.* McGraw-Hill.

Tannen, D. (2007). *You just don't understand: Women and men in conversation.* Harper Collins.

Thinking Some More

1. In this chapter, we talk about language being abstract, complex, and implicit. Can you define each of these terms with or without reference to language? For example, what does it mean for something to be abstract? Complex? Implicit? What does it mean for language in particular to be abstract?

2. It surprises many people when we say that textbook rules aren't real. They sure seem real to teachers and students! What we mean, of course, is that what winds up in our heads bears no resemblance to any rule on a page. It just *seems* like textbook rules are real to us because we've been led to believe that's the case. Can you think of things people may have been led to believe about the way the natural world works, only to find out they'd been misled (or they misinterpreted something)? What about these concepts?

    - the structure of atoms
    - the nature of gravity
    - how evolution works

3. One of the generally overlooked aspects of language is that we know not only what is possible in language but also what is impossible or not permissible. In this chapter, we saw this with the *re-* example (e.g., *do* and *redo*, but not *sleep* and **resleep*). We also saw that we can contract *want* and *to* to *wanna* and *I* and *have* to *I've* as in the first two examples below. But we also know we cannot contract them in the third and fourth examples

    a. Who do you want to invite to the party? → Who do you wanna invite to the party?
    b. I have done it. → I've done it.
    c. Who do you want to tell John the bad news? → *Who do you wanna tell John the bad news?
    d. Should I have done it? → *Should I've done it?

    No one ever teaches native speakers this when they are growing up, yet they have this knowledge. Now one ever teaches nonnative speakers this, but they, too, show nativelike intuitions and say the third and fourth examples don't sound right. This is an example of coming to know more than what you are exposed to or could have been taught and of implicit knowledge about language. Have you ever thought about this phenomenon before, that you have implicit knowledge about what is *impossible* in language? Have you ever thought about how such knowledge develops? How do you come to know what is impossible if no one teaches you?

4. At one point, we demonstrated how languages have word order based on phrases. A language can have phrases that are head-complement (e.g., English) or complement-head (e.g., Japanese). What this means is that languages that we tend to think of as being vastly different from each other can share a basic, abstract feature and be more alike than we think. Here are some examples:

   a. head-complement: English, Chinese, Russian, French
   b. complement-head: Japanese, Persian, Classical Latin, Hindi

   Try this exercise with your friends. Ask them, "Which languages are more alike, English and Latin or English and Chinese?" or "What's more alike, Japanese and Latin or Japanese and Chinese?" How do they answer? Do they even think of word order and underlying phrase structure?

5. One idea that emerged in this chapter is that communication and language are distinct concepts. Communication involves behavior, while language is a mental construct. Communication can make use of language but doesn't always have to do so. For each concept below, how many ways can you think of to express its meaning without using language?

   - No.
   - Huh? What you'd say?
   - I love you.
   - I'm ticked off at you.

6. One conclusion a person could make based on the reading just this chapter is that language is a mental construct, but communication is a social construct. Do you agree? If so, why? What do you think this claim tries to capture?

7. As we will see later in this book, second language learners also develop an abstract, complex, and independent mental representation of the language

they are acquiring. At this point, which of the following statements do you think is true?

a. Learners get explicit rules and practice them, and these rules turn into implicit mental representation.
b. Learners develop an implicit system independently of learning explicit rules and practicing them.

Is there another scenario you can envision?

Considering the Classroom

1. A recurring theme in this chapter is that the rules and structures presented in language textbooks are not psychologically real. In other words, they are not what wind up in learners' heads. What implications do you see for teaching in terms of using textbooks? As a follow-up question, imagine a publisher comes to you for input and feedback for developing a new textbook. Does anything in this chapter offer ideas about changes you'd like to see in such a book?

2. If what learners create in their heads is an abstract, complex, and implicit linguistic system that does not resemble textbook rules and structures, do you think it is necessary for learners to state rules and have explicit knowledge about language? Do you think this should be a goal of language classes?

3. Examine several introductory textbooks in the language that you (will) teach that claim to be communication oriented or proficiency based. Are they more focused on language or communication, or are they balanced? How would you determine this?

4. Veteran teachers working with proficiency-based and communicative classrooms argue about the role of grammar in their teaching. Some say it's "a pillar" in the curriculum, some say it gets in the way of focusing on communication in the classroom, and others fall in between. What is your reaction based on this chapter? We will raise this issue again later after you've read more about acquisition and research on instruction.

FAQs

If you'd like, go to Chapter 5, "Frequently Asked Questions," and check out the following questions that are related to topics in this chapter. (The numbers match the numbers for the questions in Chapter 5.)

1. Are some languages more difficult to learn than others?
2. What makes some structures difficult and some easy to acquire?
3. Aren't different parts of language learned differently?

2

Chapter 2

Ordered Development

Language develops in an ordered way. This order is not determined by a curriculum or learners' conscious efforts to acquire language.

Before You Read

Consider these statements, then come back after reading this chapter to see if your thoughts have changed.

- Students learn grammatical concepts according to the order in which those concepts are presented in the classroom or in textbooks.
- A learner's first language (L1) determines how the learner will acquire a second language (L2).
- Every learner will acquire language in his or her own unique way.
- L2 acquisition is fundamentally different from L1 acquisition.

Before we talk about language acquisition, let's talk about tadpoles and frogs. For the first 4 weeks of a tadpole's life, it has no legs or teeth and can only eat algae. At Week 7, it is still confined to water, but it begins to grow legs, starting with the back legs. At Week 14, the tadpole's lungs and front legs have developed, allowing it to venture onto land, but it still has a tail. Finally, around Week 16, its tail is no longer visible, and the metamorphosis is complete. Like almost all staged development, the tadpole's development is constrained and pre-programmed. Once that frog egg is laid, its future is mapped out (see Figure 2.1).

Figure 2.1. Tadpole Development

You might be wondering what the development of a tadpole has to do with language acquisition. We don't often think about it, but staged development is a fundamental part of nature. Just as the development of a tadpole becoming a frog is ordered and constrained, so is language acquisition, as we will see in a moment. Language is shaped and constrained by nature somehow, largely because it is something that only humans have. You may recall from Chapter 1 that we can distinguish between language and communication. Many animals communicate using movements, noises, vibrations, and pheromones, among other devices, but no animals have a system of communication that uses something as abstract and complex as human language.

Nature has a way of shaping and constraining all aspects of life. We refer to this as *ordered development*. The objective of this chapter is to provide a glimpse of how the acquisition of a second language (L2) system reflects ordered development, with predictable stages and certain constraints.

Before we begin, let's remind ourselves of an important and often overlooked fact about acquisition, whether it involves first language (L1) or L2 acquisition. Acquisition takes time. The average child spends about 14,000 hours engaged in language acquisition by the beginning of kindergarten—and the system is still not completely adultlike. Some aspects of language aren't in place until the child hits middle school, or even later. L2 acquisition also takes time, and the ordered development discussed in this chapter is not reflected in the number of semesters or classroom contact hours. Instead, the research shows that development spans years, with thousands of hours involved, as in the case of L1 acquisition. Additionally, learners don't acquire, for example, the present tense and then move on to the past tense. They are acquiring both at the same time, with parts of the present tense entering their mental representation for language while parts of the past tense enter as well. Thus, as we will see, ordered development is not a fast-moving phenomenon, and it doesn't take place in chunks. Instead, it is slow and piecemeal.

Morpheme Orders

One of the first areas to be researched in contemporary L2 acquisition involved the ordered development of morphemes, which we might consider foundational for learning. A morpheme is the smallest unit of language that carries meaning. For example, the word *hat* is a morpheme that has the meaning of a thing that is worn on someone's head. But not all morphemes are words. Let's look at the word *hats*. The *-s* on the end is another morpheme that carries the meaning of "more than one." So, when *hat* is combined with *-s*, the combination of both morphemes means "more than one hat."

Morphemes can also be added to verbs to indicate tense, person, number, mood, and a number of other meanings. Let's take the verb *walk*. This word consists of only one morpheme and means using one's legs to move from one location to another. However, if we add the morpheme *-ed*, meaning "happened in the past," we get another word consisting of two morphemes: *walked*. Similarly, we can emphasize that the action is in progress at a particular time happening by adding *-ing*: *walking* (e.g., "I am walking" or "I was walking").

Researchers of child L1 acquisition discovered ordered development of morphemes in the 1960s. Roger Brown's work on L1 English showed that children acquired verb-related morphemes in a universal order: *-ing* followed by past tense *-ed* followed by irregular past (e.g., *ate, went*), followed by third-person *-s* (e.g., "He walks"), for example. Researchers such as Heidi Dulay, Marina Burt, and Stephen Krashen subsequently examined morpheme orders in L2 English during the 1970s and also found a consistent order of acquisition for morphemes that did not seem dependent on learners' context of learning, L1, or age. Subsequent research by scholars such as Teresa Pica showed that whether learners acquired English with or without instruction, the orders were the same. Additionally, the morpheme orders in L2 acquisition largely overlapped with those in L1 acquisition. For instance, in both L1 and L2 English, the verb-related morpheme orders we just described are identical.

Researchers found a consistent order of acquisition for morphemes that did not seem to be dependent on learners' context of acquisition, L1, or age.

Findings on morpheme orders in L1 and L2 English were largely corroborated over several decades. By the early 1990s, dozens of studies seemed to replicate the findings of the early research, leading some scholars to conclude that there is a universal or natural order to morpheme acquisition. Only in one instance has it been shown that the L1 might affect ordered development of morphemes—and in a very restricted way. Zoe Pei-sui Luk and Yasuhiro Shirai compared the development of English morphemes among L2 learners who had different L1s, specifically Japanese and Spanish, and found that the order of acquisition of noun-related morphemes (e.g., plural marking, possessive marking) was different depending on whether learners' L1 was Japanese or Spanish. However, the ordered development of verb-related morphemes (e.g., *-ing*, past tense, third-person singular) was not affected by the L1 of learners. Japanese and Spanish speakers, with radically different verb-related morpheme systems in their L1s, acquired English verb-related morphemes in the same order as everyone else.

While there remains some work to be done to understand certain fine-grained elements of morpheme acquisition in English, the fact that there *is* a predictable order of acquisition is the main takeaway. Both L1 and L2 learners show evidence of this phenomenon with or without instruction, and this suggests there is something internal to the human mind that pushes learners to develop language in a particular way.

You might be wondering about languages other than English. Comparatively little research has been done on morpheme orders in other languages. A few studies have examined the L2 development of morphemes in languages that make use of many different verb-related morphemes, such as Spanish, German, and Swedish. Let's look at something different: the acquisition of case in Russian, based on research by Natalia Cherepovskaia and her colleagues.

Like Classical Latin and other languages, Russian has an elaborate case system. Nouns change their form (usually by altering an ending) depending on the grammatical function that they have in the sentence. English doesn't have case on nouns but does indicate case on pronouns. *Bill* is always *Bill* whether the noun is a subject or an object. However, only *I* can be a subject and only *me* can be an object with simple subjects and objects (e.g., "I saw Bill" versus "Bill saw me"). (We saw in Chapter 1 with compound subjects that this distinction is not so clear cut.) Looking at Russian, all of the words below can be translated to *library* in English, but each has a different ending based on its grammatical case.

biblioteк**a** (nominative case—subject of sentence)
Example: The library is big.
bibliotek**i** (genitive case—possession)
Example: the library's collections
bibliotek**e** (dative case—indirect object)
Example: I donated a book to the library.
bibliotek**u** (accusative case—direct object)
Example: I see the library.
bibliotek**oj** (instrumental case—instrument)
Example: I'm behind the library.
bibliotek**e** (locative case—location)
Example: I am at the library.

With apologies to our colleagues in Russian, the overview of cases provided is simplified for our purposes here. Apart from the nominative case, which is used almost exclusively to denote the subject of a sentence, all of the other cases have multiple uses. In fact, the genitive case can have up to 23 different uses in Russian. What is more, there are different classes of nouns that influence what the case ending looks like, as does the gender of the noun. For many contexts, native Russian speakers might not be able to explain precisely why they are using a specific case—they just *know* what form of the word sounds right. But with six different cases and all the possible forms, how do learners of Russian acquire them? It turns out that the acquisition of Russian case also exhibits ordered development.

Cherepovskaia and her colleagues looked at the written production of L2 learners at different proficiency levels and established the following ordered development for Russian case.

nominative → locative → accusative → genitive → instrumental → dative

Some aspects of this order dovetail with child L1 acquisition in Russian, such as nominative before anything else and accusative being acquired earlier rather than later. Nonetheless, the study offers a starting point to examine how a complex set of morphemes such as case in Russian is acquired, suggesting that there is probably ordered development for case marking on nouns in other languages (e.g., Classical Latin, German, Turkish). To be sure, all of the learners in the Cherepovskaia study had Spanish and Catalan as their first languages, and neither language marks case on nouns, so we can't say their order is universal. But it does suggest that learners without case marking on nouns in their L1 will most likely exhibit similar, if not identical, ordered development when acquiring Russian.

The research on Russian suggests there is probably ordered development for case marking on nouns in other languages (e.g., Classical Latin, German, Turkish).

Quick Reflection

Do you think there are implications for teaching based on morpheme order research? Is it reasonable or unreasonable to expect textbooks and resources to follow such natural orders in the presentation of material? Explain.

What else do we know about morpheme acquisition? Here are two other universal tendencies in L2 acquisition that are well established in the research.

- Singular forms are acquired before plural forms. This is true for nouns, adjectives, and verbs, for example. In Spanish, for instance, pluralization of adjectives occurs after learners acquire basic adjective position with singular nouns—and learners will often use singular adjectives in place of plural adjectives. In terms of verbs in Spanish, learners begin with bare verbs such as *come* 'eat' and *toma* 'drink' and may use these for a long time with all people and numbers (e.g., *Yo come mucho* 'I eat a lot'). Subsequently, the singulars creep in for first and second person: *como* 'I eat,' *tomo* 'I drink,' *comes* 'you eat,' *tomas* 'you drink.' Later, the plural forms come in: *comen* 'they eat,' *comemos* 'we eat,' and so on. This phenomenon is seen in languages other than Spanish as well.

- If a language has gender, learners tend to acquire one grammatical gender first and overuse it. Then they acquire the other genders in some ordered way. This is true for both nouns and agreement with nouns. In Spanish and French, for example, acquisition of masculine gender precedes feminine; as learners acquire feminine forms, they tend to make non-native structures using masculine as the default or fallback form (e.g., **La maison est grand*). In languages with more than one gender, such as German and Swahili, we see similar patterns with a default "first" gender and ordered development of the other forms over time.

In a Nutshell ...

Morphemes (e.g., pieces and parts of words that carry meaning, such as *-ing, -ed,* and *-s*) are acquired in particular orders over time. In short, "X" precedes "Y," which in turn precedes "Z" during the development of language.

It seems that a learner's L1 has little influence on the acquisition of morphemes, at least when it comes to the order in which morphemes are acquired. Do you think this means there is no influence of the L1 on acquisition? What do you think about the following statement: There is L1 influence on L2 acquisition, but it is constrained. (Note: This topic will resurface in this chapter.)

In sum, when we look at tiny parts of language such as morphemes, there is something internal to the learner that drives language acquisition in particular ways. We observe ordered development such that things line themselves up over time: Something is acquired before something else, which in turn is acquired before something else. What is more, as we will see in Chapter 4, there is little to no influence on such ordered development from instruction.

Stages of Acquisition

In this section, we will review what have been traditionally called *stages of acquisition* or *developmental sequences*. These stages reflect the acquisition of a particular structure or a singular linguistic phenomenon as opposed to morpheme orders, where researchers have looked at the ordering of different elements over time. Stages of acquisition typically look at sentence-level phenomena, but not always.

Before we dive into stages, an important research point needs to be made. Scholars do not use paper-and-pencil tests such as those that teachers might use to assess learner knowledge. Instead, scholars in both L1 and L2 acquisition gather data from various sources that are better at tapping what learners are doing without thinking. These include, but are not limited to, free and unscripted conversations and interactions, certain kinds of elicited imitation tasks that place burdens on the learner's linguistic system, and, more recently, what are called psycholinguistic techniques such as self-paced reading and eye-tracking. In the latter two cases, one might measure learners' unconscious eye movements while they read for meaning or the rate at which they move from one part of a sentence to another. We raise this issue because teachers often say they don't see ordered development, and in some cases they don't believe it exists. More than likely, this is due to what they measure: conscious knowledge of textbook rules and grammar via paper-and-pencil testing or learner speech that is heavily monitored (i.e., careful and self-edited). Researchers are not interested in such knowledge. They aim to tap what learners know unconsciously (see Chapter 1) or do unconsciously.

L2 Negation

A widely studied topic in L2 research has been how learners from different languages acquire negation. Conceptually, negation is simple. Any parent of a 2-year-old can tell you one of a toddler's favorite words: *no!* In other words, we see that there is a clear communicative desire to negate at a very young age. However, it turns out that learning to use negation in sentences involves a slow, stagelike process because negators such as *no* and *not* interact with other parts of the sentence structure, such as verbs and auxiliary verbs. It takes both L1 and L2 learners a while to sort out exactly where the negators fit in sentences of varying complexity.

In 2010, Christine Dimroth created a summary of research on the L2 development of negation cross-linguistically. The studies included data from people who learned with traditional instruction, as well as those who learned without traditional instruction, thus providing clear evidence that ordered development is not context dependent. The participants in these studies did not all have the same L1s. Four common stages are evident. Let's look at these four stages in L2 English, French, and German.

Stage 1: Negation with Nouns

Verbs are usually omitted, and a simple negator is used before the noun.

- L2 English: *__No__ beer
- L2 French: *__(Ne) pas__ bière
- L2 German: *__Nix__ Bier

Stage 2: Negation with Lexical (Main) Verbs

A lexical verb is used with a preverbal negator.

- L2 English: *I **no** drink beer.
- L2 French: *Je (ne) **pas** boire bière.
- L2 German: *Ich **nix** trinken Bier.

Stage 3: Negation with Modal/Auxiliaries

A modal verb such as *can* appears before the negator, which is targetlike in all languages.

- L2 English: I ca**n't** drink beer.
- L2 French: Je (ne) peux **pas** boire de bière.
- L2 German: Ich kann **kein** trinken Bier.

Stage 4: Negation with a Postverbal Negator

This is only relevant for French and German because English does not use postverbal negators except after auxiliaries. Note that main verbs in French or German do not need to be accompanied by an auxiliary verb like *do*.

- L2 French: Je (ne) bois **pas** de bière. 'I don't drink beer.'
- L2 German: Ich trinke **kein** Bier. 'I don't drink beer.'

It's clear that learners develop their own simplified system of negation that is not directly based on either exposure to language or to learning grammar rules. In other words, the non-nativelike sentences shown in Stages 1 and 2 are not produced by language teachers or adult native speakers, so learners are not simply mimicking what they hear or what they read. There must be some internal force that drives L2 learners to use a simplified and cross-linguistically similar system of negation and to create more complex negation as they move through the stages.

> It's clear that learners develop their own simplified system of negation that is not directly based on either exposure to language or to learning grammar rules.

For the record, the stages of negation for L2 learners look almost identical to what has been found in L1 acquisition. This research began in the 1960s in English, for example, and has been extended to other languages. What has been found generally is that the first stage involves a negator external to the other components of the sentence:

No soap.
Not a teddy bear.

In the next stage, the negator moves into the sentence, but mostly with main verbs, and the negator is preverbal:

You no do this.
He don't know how.

In the next stage, modals enter the system and the child places the negator in its adultlike spot:

You can't do this.
He won't like it.

Later in that same stage, the use of *do* as an auxiliary comes under full control, and we see adultlike negation:

He doesn't want to.
I didn't do it.

Again, similar stages have been found for children learning languages as different as French and Arabic.

A few comments about the developmental stages above are in order. First, learners do not tend to move through stages with abrupt transitions. It is better to think of acquisition as a slow gradient climb to the top of a hill. Going back to the tadpole example for a moment, let's think about when that tadpole first gets legs. It doesn't happen overnight; the tadpole doesn't go to sleep on Monday night and suddenly wake up with legs on Tuesday morning. And once the tadpole has legs and even lungs, there is still a tail, something that has lingered since the early stages of development. The acquisition of negation shows something similar. For example, a novice learner's system of negation may seem to largely reflect Stage 1, but at some point, elements of Stage 2 will emerge, while elements of Stage 1 linger. It would be unusual, however, for a learner to vacillate between Stages 1 and 4, just like it would be almost impossible for a tadpole to leap from its initial stage of no legs and teeth to a fully formed frog. Think of stages as overlapping ovals as in Figure 2.2.

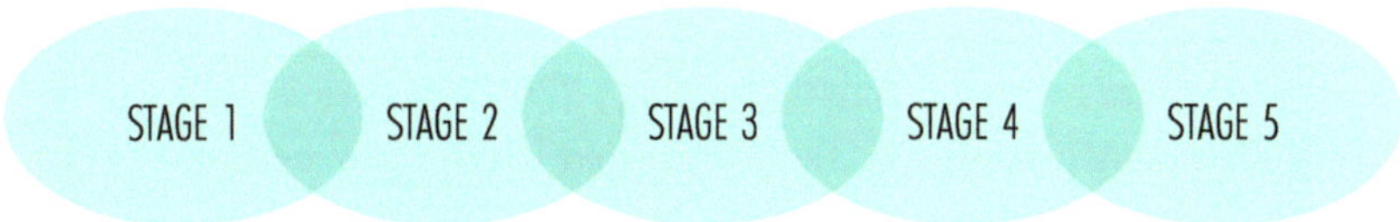

Figure 2.2. Stages of Learning

A second important note about stages is that learners exhibit different rates of development. Some may never pass through the more advanced stages if they do have sufficient exposure to language (something we will discuss in Chapter 3). Others may pass through the stages more quickly if they are immersed in the language. It is important to note, though, that even learners who move through the stages more quickly do not skip any stages. For instance, even the most successful L2 learners do not start at Stage 3 or 4 of acquiring negation. Nevertheless, it is possible for these learners to move through Stages 1 and 2 quickly, giving the illusion that they are skipping stages. As researchers and teachers, we might sometimes miss what a learner knows or does because we simply didn't see it, may not have been looking for it, or got to the learner too late to see it.

Quick Reflection

The issue of reacting to learners' errors will be addressed in more depth in Chapter 5. However, based on what you've learned so far, do you think correcting learners' non-native production influences ordered development? How do you think teachers should respond to a learner when that learner uses something like a Stage 2 structure in negation? How would you respond in the classroom?

Ser *and* Estar *in Spanish*

An additional example of staged development has been extensively documented focuses on verbs of being in Spanish. The two main Spanish verbs that translate as "be" are *ser* and *estar*. In the majority of contexts, these verbs are not interchangeable. For example, the verb *ser* is used to link noun phrases with other noun phrases or adjectives: *Bill* ***es*** *profesor* 'Bill is a professor' or *Bill* ***es*** *amable* 'Bill is nice.' The verb *estar*, on the other hand, can be used to describe progressive actions, locations, or certain physical and emotional states: *Terry* ***está*** *corriendo* 'Terry is running'; *Terry* ***está*** *en casa* 'Terry is at home'; *Terry* ***está*** preocupada 'Terry is worried.' Both verbs are frequent in Spanish and among the first verbs that learners are exposed to, yet research shows they are difficult to acquire. Bill VanPatten's research in the 1980s revealed that L2 Spanish learners show ordered development in the acquisition of these two verbs. In a 2010 review of all the research to date, VanPatten describes four documented stages:

Stage 1: Omission. In this stage, L2 learners often omit verbs of being completely.

*Bill profesor.

*Terry preocupada.

Stage 2: Overuse of *ser*. Learners begin to use verbs of being but predominantly use *ser*. The verb *estar* is largely absent but may be used in what are called *chunked expressions*.

Bill **es** profesor.

*Terry **es** preocupada.

A chunked expression might be *¿Cómo estás?* 'How are you?'

Stage 3: *Estar* used as auxiliary verb. In this stage, *estar* is used as an auxiliary to describe progressive actions.

Terry **está** corriendo.

Stage 4: *Estar* used as copular verb. *Estar* is used as a copular verb to describe location and certain physical and emotional states.

Terry **está** en casa.

Tery **está** preocupada.

The first stage of acquisition—omission—might seem surprising. L2 Spanish learners certainly never hear native speakers or their teachers say verb-less sentences such as *Bill profesor*, so they cannot be picking up what they hear or see. Omission might also be surprising to some because the learners in many of the studies were native English speakers. In standard American English, native speakers do not omit verbs of "being" (that is, we don't say "*Bill not tall"), so why would they do it in a second language? As it turns out, such omission is common in early stages of both L1 and L2 acquisition; also, some languages (e.g., Mandarin) don't require verbs like *be*. In Mandarin, it is correct to say *Bǐ'ěr bù gāo* 'Bill not tall.'

In research on *ser* and *estar* since the 1980s, the overall pattern of ordered development has stood the test of time when looking at classroom and non-classroom learners whose first languages are English, Korean, and Chinese. The research has revealed some finer-grained analyses of some of the stages, but the stages themselves have held.

In a Nutshell ...

So far, we have seen two examples of stages of acquisition or developmental sequences. One involves negation, for which there is research on a variety of languages. A second stage is the acquisition of *ser* and *estar*. It is important to point out that stages and sequences are context independent—that is, both classroom and non-classroom learners are observed to traverse such stages. And, as in the case of morpheme orders, learners' L1s do not determine the sequences or stages.

(cont.)

What does the existence of stages of acquisition or developmental sequences suggest to you? Would you conclude that somehow the brain is hardwired to acquire language in certain ways or that most instruction is inadequate and perhaps better explanations of language and better practice are needed?

Relative Clauses

Sentences can be simple or complex. A simple sentence has a single main verb, such as in "Bill is friends with Terry" or "Bill has visited Chile" (*visit* is the main verb and *has* is an auxiliary). A complex sentence tends to have more than one main verb and often a clause marker such as *that, who, which*, and so on, as in "Bill thinks that Terry needs a vacation" or "Bill is the is the guy who writes fiction." Forming embedded sentences of what are often called *subordinate clauses* is one of the most complex stages of sentence building. Relative clauses are a type of subordinate clause that has received considerable attention in both L1 and L2 research. Relative clauses modify nouns. There are six different types of relative clauses that linguists discuss, and they are organized in what is known as an *implicational hierarchy*:

1. *Subject:* The relative clause modifies the subject of a sentence (e.g., "Jack is the person who bought the cookies.").
2. *Object:* The relative clause modifies the object of a sentence (e.g., Jack ate the cookies that Sam made.").
3. *Indirect object:* The relative clause describes the indirect object of a sentence (e.g., "Jack is the person who Sam sold the cookies to.").
4. *Oblique:* The relative clause describes the object of a preposition (e.g., "Jack is the person who Sam told us about.").
5. *Genitive:* The relative clause describes possession of something (e.g., "Sam is the person whose cookies Jack bought.").
6. *Object of comparison:* The relative clause describes an object of comparison (e.g., "Jack is the person who Sam is a better cook than.").

Not all languages have all six types of relative clauses. All languages have subject relative clauses, but not all have object, indirect object, oblique, genitive, or object of comparison clauses. However, if a language *does* have a certain type of relative clause, it is expected to have all the types above it on the hierarchy as well. So, if a language has indirect object relative clauses, we assume it has subject and object relative clauses as well, but we could not assume it has oblique, genitive, or object of comparison relative clauses.

So, what do we know about this hierarchy and the acquisition of relative clauses? First, ordered development does seem to be reflected by the implicational hierarchy. In English, for example, a language in which all six types of clauses exist, it is well documented that L2 learners—regardless of their L1—find subject relative clauses easier than object relative clauses, which in turn are easier than indirect relative clauses, and so on. When we say the learners find such clauses to be easier, we mean the learners use a certain relative clause more than others (some may be absent in their production) and make fewer non-native structures with that relative clause compared to others. The research also shows that no learner is better at using clauses lower on the hierarchy than they are at using clauses that are higher.

An interesting finding in the research on relative clause formation is that learners have a universal tendency to use what are called *resumptive pronouns* inside the relative clause. A resumptive pronoun duplicates the function of relative clause marker *what* or *who*, as in the following example:

(1) That is the man who I talked to. → That is the man who I talked to him.

In this example, the pronoun *him* replicates the function of indirect object of the verb. Resumptive pronouns are not allowed in languages like English, Spanish, Italian, and others for relative clauses, although they are allowed in languages such as Arabic. What has been found in L2 research is that many learners readily insert and accept sentences as possible with resumptive pronouns when acquiring relative clauses, regardless of whether or not their L1 allows them to do so and whether or not they receive instruction.

Interestingly, another non-nativelike developmental structure with relative clauses is to replicate a full noun instead of a pronoun. For some learners, a preferred "strategy" is to produce sentences similar to the following examples:

(2) That is the man who I talked to. → That is the man who I talked to the man.
(3) Bill is the author who Russ knows. → Bill is the author who Russ knows Bill.

It seems that how the L1 forms relative clauses can't account for what learners do during development.

In short, a universal tendency in the acquisition of relative clauses is for learners to pass through a stage in which they duplicate the function of the relative clause marker somewhere inside the relative clause itself. It seems that learners' internal systems don't want to leave a gap inside the relative clause and that how the L1 forms relative clauses can't account for what learners do during development.

Research on the acquisition of relative clauses in other L2s is scarce, but there is some research on Spanish, Arabic, and East Asian languages. The implicational hierarchy sometimes predicts ordered development, but not always. For example, in languages like Mandarin and Korean, the implicational hierarchy is not the best predictor of ease or difficulty, with other factors seemingly at work. Nonetheless, there is ordered development in the acquisition of relative clauses in these languages. That ordered development just needs an explanation different from that found for English and Spanish, for example. Thus, ordered development is sometimes universal or close to it, as in the case of negation, and other times there is ordered development within a given language or language families. Explaining such differences is not the point of this book. Our goal, rather, is to alert teachers and others that ordered development exists, and as we will see in Chapter 4, such development exists independently of instruction.

Quick Reflection

Do you think the acquisition of relative clauses is more important for speaking or writing? Or is it equally important for both?

Tense and Aspect in the Past

Another area in L2 research that has received considerable attention is how learners acquire what is called the tense-aspect system. Tense refers to relative time period, the major ones being present, past, and future. Aspect refers to how an event is viewed or reported, such as whether it began or ended at a particular point in time (e.g., "Bill stood when the judge arrived"), was in progress at a particular point (e.g., "Bill was standing as the judge entered"), or was something habitual (e.g., "Bill typically stood when the judge entered"). Tense-aspect systems can be complex because of the nature of verbs. Without getting into too much detail, events can be of two major types: telic events (those that are instantaneous, such as "blink" and "slam shut", and those that have an end point, such as "run a mile" or "draw a circle") and atelic events (those that represent activities without end points, such as "run" and "eat," and those that represent states such as "be tall," "desire," and "think").

Learners show a strong tendency to first limit the simple past tense to certain types of telic events or events that have a clear end point.

In terms of ordered development, learners across the board with different languages and from different L1s show a strong tendency to first limit the simple past tense to certain types of telic events or events that have a clear end point (e.g., "I finished my homework" or "Bill wrote a story"). When they first use the past tense to indicate something ongoing, they tend to do so with certain kinds of atelic verbs (e.g., "Bill was a professor" or "I thought about it"). Only in subsequent stages do we see learners develop the ability to use grammatical means to indicate completion of a durative event (e.g., "Bill was a professor until 2018") or the ongoing nature of certain kinds of telic events (e.g., "I was standing up [in the process of standing up] when I heard a shot").

We don't want to get too much into the details of the acquisition of a tense-aspect system because both the theory behind tense-aspect and the research on acquisition can be daunting. We've provided some readings should you wish to dive into the complexity of this topic. We will simply say that stages of acquisition for tense-aspect have been studied with classroom and non-classroom learners with various L1s learning L2s such as English, Spanish, Japanese, Chinese, and other languages. We have included readings at the end of the chapter should you wish to get into the weeds on this complex realm of acquisition.

In a Nutshell ...

A significant area of ordered development involves how a particular structure or element is acquired. Scholars have uncovered what are called stages of acquisition or developmental sequences. The basic question the research asks is, How is "X" acquired over time? What does its evolution look like?

Consider the question we just posed: What does its evolution look like? What do you know about evolution and how it happens? Based on what you've read so far, what do you think of using the term *evolution* to describe what happens to a learner's mental representation of language over time (e.g., in a sentence such as "The learner's internal linguistic system evolves over time."). In what ways is this process similar to and different from something like natural evolution?

Before moving on, we want to list some of the other aspects of language for which there is documented staged development. We won't describe them; we just want to point out that there are many such areas that have been studied. The list is merely suggestive, not exhaustive.

- the acquisition of question formation (e.g., with *wh*- words, such as "Where does Bill live?" and "Why won't Terry speak to me?")
- the acquisition of the sound system—for example, how learners acquire consonant clusters at the ends of words and syllables, especially when their L1s don't have such clusters (e.g., [ks] as in *makes* and *takes*, [sts] as in *tests* and *nests*, [mps] as in *glimpse* and *limps*)

- vocabulary acquisition—for example, how learners acquire a particular word and all its meanings and uses (e.g., *run, run down, run over, run in your stocking, run for Congress, runny nose*)
- pragmatics, which refers to speaker intent and the devices a speaker uses to signal such intent (e.g., direct accusation: "You pushed Bill. I know you did!" vs. indirect accusation: "I wonder where you were when Bill fell."). In this area, researchers look at ordered development for direct versus indirect speech acts of such things as offering opinions, refusing, and making recommendations.

Ordered development seems to permeate most aspects of acquisition.

U-Shaped Development

As we have seen in this chapter, language acquisition tends to occur slowly and in a piecemeal fashion as different parts of the language system are put together. For parts of the language system that have defined stages like those described in the previous sections, learners will generally move through each stage on a slow trajectory toward targetlike knowledge and production, with some overlap between stages. However, occasionally a learner will exhibit what is called *U-shaped development*. U-shaped development begins with a period of high accuracy of a particular linguistic item, followed by a period of low accuracy, followed once again by a more stable period of high(er) accuracy. The high-low-high pattern resembles a "U" if plotted over time, as in Figure 2.3. Accuracy with a particular feature is indicated by the percentages on the Y axis and time periods are indicated on the X axis.

Figure 2.3. U-Shaped Development of Language

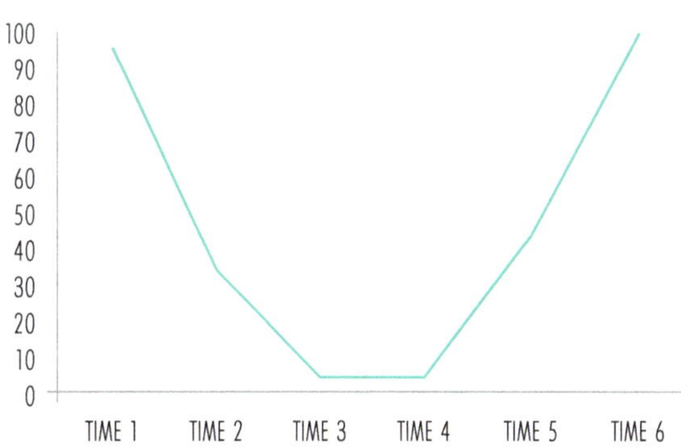

The most well-known example of U-shaped development has been observed in the English past tense. Children who are native English speakers will often produce irregular verbs such as *went* and *ate* with high accuracy as they begin to learn the past tense. These verbs are used frequently in English and are important for daily communication in children's lives, so it makes sense for them to acquire these words early. However, children begin to build a more fully formed past tense system, which is dominated by the morpheme represented by the sounds [t] or [d] or [ɪd] as in *matched*, *closed*, and *wanted*. Once children acquire regular past tense, they tend to overgeneralize those forms and apply them to all verbs, resulting in non-adultlike productions such as *goed/wented* and *eated*. During this period, their production of irregular verbs is less accurate. However, this stage of overgeneralization eventually comes to an end as learners sort out the regular verbs from the irregular ones, and they once again produce irregular verbs with high accuracy.

The phenomenon of U-shaped development has been studied more in L1 acquisition, but this same pattern can occur in an L2 as well. In fact, the U-shaped behavior with past tense acquisition has been documented in L2 learners of English. Those of us who teach Spanish are familiar with U-shaped behavior. One of the first phrases that L2 learners pick up is *No sé* 'I don't know.' The first-person singular verb form *sé* 'I know' is irregular and comes from the verb *saber*, but learners often learn this phrase before they have acquired any representation for the present tense system in Spanish. As they acquire regular present tense forms in Spanish, learners' underlying representation posits *-o* as the indicator of first-person singular, as in *como* 'I eat'; e*studio* 'I study'; *vivo* 'I live.' At this point, learners may overgeneralize this regular pattern to the irregular verb *saber* and produce the non-target form **sabo*. After a while, learners will eventually sort out the irregular verbs from the regular ones and again produce the target form, *sé* 'I know.' Incidentally, this phenomenon is documented in Spanish L1 acquisition as well.

Quick Reflection

Have you ever been fooled by students when they seem to start out doing something correctly in the language only to move into a phase where they do it incorrectly? How did you react to such behavior?

A Note About Variation

In education circles, and perhaps in society more generally, people like to stress individual differences and variation in how people think, live, or behave. In L2 research, scholars have examined variation as well. What this means for ordered development is simple. It is possible to have universal and strong tendencies in a large population of learners such that ordered development exists, while also having some individual variation within stages. Let's look at a few concrete examples.

In the acquisition of negation in English L2, Stage 2 involves the use of a subject, a main verb, and a negator before the verb, as in "I no drink beer." However, there can be variation in this stage in one of two ways. Some learners pick up the chunk *don't* and use it along with *no*, producing sentences such as "I no drink beer," "I don't like it," "Bill no writes well," and "Bill don't know." This is variation for a learner in a given stage. The basic pattern is the same, but we see alternating uses of a negator. Variation can also exist between learners such that one learner overwhelmingly favors *no* while another learner overwhelmingly favors the chunk *don't*. In short, there can be variation within a stage for a single learner or between learners in the same stage. Yet, the stage is still the same: subject + preverbal negator + main verb.

As another example, when learners begin to acquire past tense marking, they may not be consistent. As they enter the stage where, let's say, regular past tense marking comes in, we may see vacillation between nativelike forms such as *comió* in Spanish for "he/she ate" and non-native like forms, typically the present tense, as in *come* (also meaning "he/she ate").

The point of this section is to remind ourselves that ordered development and variation are both possible and can co-exist; they are not mutually exclusive. However, variation does not override ordered development. Learners don't vary, for example, in that some skip stages and some don't, or that some follow one order of stages and others don't. Variation happens within stages or at certain points in time. Interestingly, this combination of ordered development and variation is true of L1 acquisition as well. Such variation is remi-

Ordered development and variation are both possible and can co-exist. They are not mutually exclusive.

niscent of the analogy from the beginning of this chapter. When a tadpole begins to grow legs, its back legs come in first. Some tadpoles may grow their legs slightly faster than others, and some may wind up with slightly longer legs than others, but there is no subgroup of tadpoles that grows front legs first or grows lungs before back legs. That is just not the way that tadpoles develop.

Summary

Language acquisition is ordered. It has been shown repeatedly that the acquisition of different components of the linguistic system develop in a stagelike or ordered way. There is some individual variation in what learners do, but such variation tends to be limited to what occurs within a given stage. Such variation does not affect stages or ordered development in any significant way. Although language acquisition tends to follow a slow trajectory with gradual development, there are exceptions. As learners' internal systems sort out regular from irregular structures, for example, it is possible for them to experience U-shaped development. In this case, they perform in non-nativelike ways when originally they produced something in nativelike ways. And as we have seen, the learner's L1 does not seem to be the best predictor of ordered development. In fact, we see some surprising turns in learners' development that wouldn't be there if their L1s were somehow directing acquisition. As a prelude to Chapter 4, we have also alluded to the fact that instruction is not a determining factor in ordered development.

Another point we touched on in this chapter is that what happens in L2 acquisition often mirrors what happens in L1 acquisition. Both situations involve ordered development, and sometimes the specifics of the development are similar, if not identical. This does not mean that L2 acquisition and L1 acquisition are identical in all respects (this is touched on in an FAQ in Chapter 5), but it does suggest that there is some kind of learner-internal process in acquisition that both contexts share.

Ordered development has led scholars to believe that some mechanisms internal to learners are somehow guiding and constraining L2 acquisition. Scholars debate exactly what the guiding and constraining mechanisms are, but they all agree that something exists in the human mind that shapes language acquisition in predictable ways. In the next chapter, we will look at the ingredients for language acquisition and what might be the source of the constraints seen in ordered development.

Selected References and Suggested Readings

Here are specific resources mentioned in the chapter:

Cherepovskaia, N., Slioussar, N., & Denissenko Denissenko, A. (2022). Acquisition of the nominal case system in Russian as a second language. *Second Language Research, 38*(3), 555–580. https://doi.org/10.1177%2F0267658320988058

Dimroth, C. (2010). The acquisition of negation. In L. Horn (Ed.), *The expression of negation*, pp. 39–73. De Gruyter Mouton. DOI:10.1515/9783110219302.39.

Luk, Z. P. S., & Shirai, Y. (2009). Is the acquisition order of grammatical morphemes impervious to L1 knowledge? Evidence from the acquisition of plural *-s*, articles, and possessive *'s*. *Language Learning*, *59*(4), 721–754.

VanPatten, B. (2010). Some verbs are more perfect than others: Why learners have difficulty with *ser* and *estar* and what it means for instruction. *Hispania, 93*(1), 29–38.

To learn more about the stages of acquisition and developmental sequences, we suggest the following resources:

Ellis, R. (2015). *Understanding second language acquisition* (2nd ed.). Oxford University Press. (See especially Chapter 4, "The Development of a Second Language.")

Hatch, E. (Ed.). (1978). *Second language acquisition: A book of readings.* Newbury House. (This resource is a classic and contains many empirical studies of the early work on ordered development.)

Long, M. H., & Larsen-Freeman, D. (1991). *An introduction to second language acquisition research.* Longman. (This book might seem dated to some readers, but it is a gem, and Chapter 4, "Interlanguage Studies: Substantive Findings," is an excellent overview of the first 2 decades of L2 research on ordered development.)

Salaberry, M. R., & Shirai, Y. (Eds.). (2002). *The L2 acquisition of tense-aspect morphology*. John Benjamins. (This is an excellent book that contains studies on a variety of different languages. The introductory chapter on tense-aspect is useful for the first-time reader on this topic.)

In 2007, the journal *Studies in Second Language Acquisition* published a special issue on the acquisition and processing of relative clauses that included research from a variety of languages that might be of interest. Here is an article about a foundational study of the non-effects of instruction for relative clauses, along with learners' tendency to insert resumptive or full nouns inside a relative clause:

Pavesi, M. (1986). Markedness, discoursal modes, and relative clause formation in a formal and an informal context. *Studies in Second Language Acquisition, 8*(1), 38–55.

To learn about ordered development in a first language, we can't help but recommend a classic that is foundational for much of the subsequent L2 acquisition scholarship:

Brown, R. (1973). *A first language: The early stages.* Harvard University Press. (This book is now available through a partnership with DeGruyter. You can find it on the Harvard University Press website.)

Finally, we recommend this book, which gathers together foundational essays and empirical research in L1 acquisition:

Lust, B., & Foley, C. (2003). *First language acquisition: The essential readings*. Wiley Blackwell.

Thinking Some More

1. Return to the "Before You Read" box at the beginning of the chapter. What do you think of the statements now? Has your mind changed about any of the topics?
2. An early hypothesis about L2 acquisition was Stephen Krashen's Natural Order Hypothesis, which he discusses in one of his most cited publications, *Principles and Practice in Second Language Acquisition* (1982). Krashen has now made this book available online as a PDF that can be found

via a simple internet search. Read what he says about the Natural Order Hypothesis, then compare that to what you've read in this chapter. To what extent is there overlap? To what extent are there differences? Keep in mind that in 1982, Krashen based his hypothesis on a limited amount of research, while today we know more about ordered development than we did then.

3. Teachers and advanced speakers of a language have difficulty reflecting on their own development and often cannot recollect their own ordered development. Why do you think this is so? Consider interviewing several people to see if they can remember their own ordered development or if, on their own, they mention anything like ordered development as they ponder their experiences.

4. Consider the acquisition of morphemes and something as simple as singular versus plural. Why does learning how to make plurals and how to make adjectives agree with plural nouns always follow singular forms? Why is an understanding of plural forms of verbs generally acquired after an understanding of singular forms? Is there something inherently more difficult or complex about plurality compared to singularity? What about gender? Why is feminine "more difficult" than masculine to acquire?

5. We began this chapter talking about tadpole-to-frog development and how it is ordered and immutable. The point of this chapter is that much of the process of language acquisition is the same. After reading this chapter, what other analogies or metaphors can you think of that capture the essences of ordered development?

6. One approach to ordered development we did not review in this chapter is captured in Manfred Pienemann's Processability Theory. Chapters 1, 3, and 4 in Pienemann and Jörg-U. Kessler's book *Studying Probability Theory* (2011) should be somewhat accessible now that you have read this chapter. Read these chapters, then prepare a statement about how Pienemann's approach fits in with the ideas in this chapter.

7. List three to five takeaways from this chapter, then discuss them with a colleague who has not read the book. What is that person's reaction?

Considering the Classroom

1. In this chapter, you saw that grammatical structures are acquired in a stagelike way. Consider the organization and content of a typical textbook. Are textbooks and textbook assessments designed in a way that acknowledges that students learn grammatical concepts along a slow trajectory, with most of the points along this trajectory characterized by non-target-like comprehension and production? Is there a different way to organize curriculum and assessments so that students' slow and stagelike acquisition is more respected?
2. Consider the following typical expectations about learners' oral production in the classroom. Do you agree with these statements? How would you address them based on the content of this chapter?
    - Learners should speak in complete sentences.
    - Learners' production should be "error free."
3. Have you ever had students who seemed to regress to an earlier stage of acquisition or exhibit U-shaped development? How did you deal with it?

FAQs

If you'd like, go to Chapter 5, "Frequently Asked Questions," and check out the following questions that are related to topics in this chapter. (The numbers match the numbers for the questions in Chapter 5.)

4. What about the first language? Doesn't it cause interference?
5. What about errors? Don't learners develop bad habits if they aren't corrected?
6. Do the ACTFL Oral Proficiency Guidelines and Standards reflect ordered development?

3

Chapter 3

The Basic Ingredients

Language acquisition involves both internal and external ingredients. Both are important. But the importance of internal ingredients tends to get ignored.

Before You Read

Consider these statements, then come back after reading this chapter to see if your thoughts have changed.

- Motivation clearly guides second language acquisition.
- Some ingredients in acquisition are more important than others.
- Learners have something inside their heads that governs the course of language acquisition.
- A key ingredient in acquisition is practice.

Anybody who's followed a recipe knows there are two parts to the recipe: the ingredients and the preparation or procedure. Ingredients are listed with their quantities, such as how much flour, butter, or salt. Preparation is set up as a step-by-step procedure using verbs such as *preheat*, *combine*, *stir in*, *beat*, *add*, and *bake*. The acquisition of language also has ingredients and something like a procedure, although unlike in a recipe, nothing is really specified in terms of quantity and step-by-step instructions. Acquisition is a bit more complex than, say, baking a cake. In this chapter, we will review the basic ingredients for acquisition.

In terms of language acquisition, we can talk about the basic ingredients falling into two broad categories: internal and external. By *internal*, we mean mechanisms in the learner's mind that work on language. By *external*, we mean things that aren't these mechanisms. The best way to make this distinction clear is to jump right into a discussion of things that are internal to learners. But a note is in order first. Because this book is meant to be brief, introductory, and reader friendly, our treatment of the basic ingredients in acquisition will necessarily be cursory and selective. There are lots of big, thick books out there for readers who want to get into the weeds on issues raised in this chapter and to explore beyond the basics. We have listed some at the end of the chapter.

Internal Ingredients

There are two internal categories of mechanisms scholars have examined to study language acquisition. One category of mechanisms is called *language-specific mechanisms*. In this category, the mechanisms work on language only, using a particular kind of data for building a linguistic system. Another category can be called *general learning mechanisms*. These mechanisms work on all kinds of stimuli, allowing us to learn such things as the difference between a dog and a cat and how to read sheet music. We will look at language-specific mechanisms first.

Language-Specific Mechanisms

Language-specific mechanisms are traceable to the influential work of Noam Chomsky, dating back to the 1960s and continuing to this day. He posited the idea of some internal device that is unique to humans and operates solely on language data. In the 1990s, he launched the idea of what is now called *Universal Grammar*, or UG for short. In mainstream linguistic theoretical circles, UG governs the shape of natural human languages. The basic role of UG is to make sure that a language is learnable by any human child who doesn't have impairments. As such, all human languages must obey whatever is contained in UG. Under current accounts, UG itself is minimal yet powerful. It consists of a small set of *operations*, a small set of *principles*, and a limited set of *abstract features*. We will offer examples of each to illustrate what we mean with these terms. A brief word of caution: Much of linguistic theory can be very technical and use highly specific terms and constructs. We will do our best to keep the basic ideas as accessible as possible.

The basic role of UG is to make sure that a language is learnable by any unimpaired human child.

One example of a basic operation in UG is called Merge. This operation allows words to combine and form phrases, such that *man* and *with a beard* merge to form a noun phrase "man with a beard" written as [$_{NP}$ man with a beard]. In turn, *the* can be merged with *man with a beard* to form a determiner phrase: "the man with a beard." The result is one phrase nestled inside another: [$_{DP}$ the [$_{NP}$ man with a beard]]. And this can be merged with a verb such as *see* to create a verb phrase, again with more nesting: [$_{VP}$ see [$_{DP}$ the [$_{NP}$ man with a beard]]].

Another basic operation is Move, which allows for constituents in sentences to move around—under certain conditions, of course. Thus, with questions in English using *which, what, how, who,* and other question words, Move allows for these elements to leave their place of origin and land in some predetermined spot in the sentence. For example, "Bill saw who?" becomes "Who did Bill see?" The word *who* leaves its object position behind the verb to move elsewhere. We will touch on this a bit later when we talk about something called a Q feature.

Quick Reflection

Do you think learners need to be taught that things move in sentences (i.e., do they need to be taught that something like *what* might have originated as an object of a verb)? Were you ever taught this in your first or second language (assuming those languages have movement of something like *wh* words)?

An example of a principle in UG is that sentences are built on phrases and all phrases have a head and a complement. We saw phrases earlier when talking about Merge and we also saw them in Chapter 1 when we compared English and Japanese. In the examples we just used, the verb phrase consists of the head *see* and its complement *the man with the beard.* The determiner phrase consists of the head *the* and its complement *man with the beard.* The noun phrase consists of *man* and the complement *with the beard.* And so on. Some languages are head + complement, like English, Chinese, and French. Others are complement + head, like Japanese, Turkish, and Classical Latin. So, languages can vary on two dimensions when it comes to basic word order, and head and complement order is the foundation for basic word order in all languages.

A second example of a principle in UG is the Extended Projection Principle. This principle basically says that a sentence must have a subject—not an utterance, but a sentence. A sentence always has a verb, whereas an utterance does not. "Russ, are you ready?" is a sentence. "Ready?" is an utterance. So, any sentence with a verb in any language will always have a subject. However, languages can vary as to whether the subject must be visible (overt) or invisible (null). English requires visible overt subjects. For this reason, "I like Russ. *Is a very smart guy." is not allowed in English because an overt subject pronoun *he* is required: "I like Russ. He is a very smart guy." Likewise, verbs such as *rain* that have no real-world entity that can be the subject are required in English to take placeholder subjects such as *it*: "It is raining," not "*Is raining." Spanish, like many languages, does allow null subjects, so *Me gusta Russ. Es muy inteligente* and *Me gusta Russ. Él es muy inteligente* are both grammatical (although the former is more natural sounding than the latter for reasons beyond this discussion). And for verbs such as *rain*, Spanish does not allow placeholder subjects, requiring such sentences to have null subjects: *Está lloviendo,* not **Él está lloviendo*. In short, the Extended Projection Principle requires subjects in sentences, but as in the case of phrase structure, languages can vary on two dimensions: whether or not they allow null subjects.

In the case of features, not all languages select the same features, but when they do select a particular feature, there are consequences. An example is the feature Tense. When a language has this feature, it means that sentences must express tense in some formal way, usually with verb inflections, auxiliaries, or both. Standard English, for example, minimally encodes tense on verbs: "Russ eats" [present], "Russ ate" [past], "Russ will eat" [future]. Other languages with Tense as a feature include Russian, Japanese, Arabic, Classical Latin, and German, to name a few. Mandarin Chinese doesn't have Tense as a feature, thus there is no requirement for it to encode tense on verbs (although, as in any language, Chinese makes use of adverbials of time such as *yesterday* and *next week*). Thus, in Mandarin, there is only *Russ chī* 'Russ eat,' and other words do the work of indicating tense to a listener or reader (e.g., *Russ zuótiān chī le* 'Russ eat yesterday'; the particle *le* indicates something called *aspect* but does not indicate tense). Languages like Mandarin that do not have Tense as a feature include Indonesian and Vietnamese. Note that languages that have Tense do not need to mark tense in the same way. English, Spanish, and Arabic, for example, all make distinctions between past, present, and future on their verbs but do so in different ways. Yet it is the underlying feature of Tense that obligates each language to grammatically mark the three-way distinction to begin with.

A second example of a feature is called Q, which is short for *question*. A Q feature in a language causes the movement of *wh*-words (e.g., *where, why, what*) from one part of a sentence to another part. English has a Q feature and thus moves *wh-* words into a particular spot in a sentence (e.g., "Russ knows who?" → "Who does Russ know?"). It may also move auxiliaries or modals into the same spot in the case of *yes/no* questions (e.g., "Russ can explain this to me." → "Can Russ explain this to me?"). In addition, to carry tense and person-number features, English inserts the non-meaningful auxiliary *do* to make certain *yes/no* questions: "Russ lives in Ohio." → "Does Russ live in Ohio?" Spanish and French, for example, can do the same, but they don't have an auxiliary such as *do* and do not have modals such as *will* and *would*. But because Q features are tied to Tense as well, Spanish can move verbs into the spot where *do* and modal verbs are moved in English. The result is what many call *subject-verb inversion*: *Russ puede explicarme esto.* → *¿Puede Russ explicarme esto?* are equivalents to the English sentences above, but singular main verbs can do the same: *Russ explica esto bien.* → *¿Explica Russ esto bien?* 'Does Russ explain this well?' Mandarin does not have a Q feature, which is why *wh-* questions must take the form of something like *Nǐ chī le shénme?* 'You ate what?' and *Nǐ shuō shénme?* 'You're saying what?' where the *wh-* word *shénme* stays in object position behind the verb.

The components of UG, then, interact in various ways to give us natural human languages. From a small set of components, a finite but large number of combinations give us variations such as English, German, Swahili, Japanese, and Urdu. The result is that languages are much more alike than we often think, and they adhere to some abstract and deep principles. Here's an interesting example to illustrate. Japanese and Basque (spoken in northern Spain and on the edge of the Pyrennes in France) do not belong to the same language family and evolved thousands of miles apart from each other. In fact, Basque is considered a language isolate and not part of any known language family. Yet Japanese and Basque share many aspects: For example, both are complement + head, both have case marking on nouns, both have postpositions but not prepositions, both have a Q feature—and, in fact, both use a particle to mark *yes/no* questions—and so on. We certainly aren't suggesting that Basque and Japanese are identical; they are not. What we are suggesting is that in such cases, when we look beyond the surface features of language (e.g., vocabulary, word endings), we begin to see similarities across languages and how certain aspects of language seem to group together. In short, languages "behave" in certain ways. They are constrained.

To be sure, linguists debate the details and exact content of UG. With each decade, refinements are made to the theory and linguists have narrowed the scope of UG. In its current form, UG contains a smaller set of features and constraints than originally thought when the idea was first formulated many years ago. Compare this evolution to atomic theory. The current conceptualization of atoms among scientists is different than it was 100 years ago, yet the construct of *atom* still exists. And to be sure, not all people working with language adhere to generative theory (e.g., those working with Construction Grammars). However, we will let them make their case to teachers rather than speak on their behalf.

In a Nutshell ...

Universal Grammar is a language-specific mechanism that constrains the nature of linguistic representation. It does not dictate specific things (e.g., what the verb endings are in Spanish, what the modals are in English). Instead, it provides both broad (and abstract) constraints that all languages must obey, as well as a finite set of features from which languages may choose.

Earlier, we said that Japanese and Basque share a number of characteristics because both are complement + head languages, and this feature has consequences in the rest of the grammar for those languages. Most people, however, would assume that Japanese and Basque have little in common. For the average person, what do you think influences why they think languages are similar or different?

Why is UG relevant to language acquisition? The answer is relatively simple. As learners build language in their heads over time, the linguistic system is constrained and guided by UG even though the system may be non-native. For example, once a learner's linguistic system has determined that the language in question has Tense as a feature, then a series of consequences ensue (i.e., there will be some kind of grammatical representation for Tense). Once a learner's linguistic system has determined that the language has a Q feature, a different set of consequences ensues (i.e., certain grammatical devices will be used to distinguish interrogative sentences from declarative ones). And so on. Learners aren't free to create any old language they want in their heads. They unknowingly create a language that obeys basic principles and guidelines of all human languages.

As learners build language in their heads over time, the linguistic system is constrained and guided by UG.

A simple example comes from research by Bill VanPatten and Megan Smith published in 2015. In that study, completely naive learners of Japanese with no knowledge of any other complement + head language were trained on 50 simple sentences consisting of subject-object-verb (object-verb represents complement + head order for the verb phrase) and 50 sentences with postpositional particles (i.e., Japanese is complement + head, so it does not have prepositions but has postpositions, as in '(the) table on' *tēburu no* but not 'on the table' **no tēburu* —see Chapter 1). Training consisted of listening to sentences being read as an image depicting the meaning of the sentence was displayed on a computer screen. After the training session, the learners were surprised with a test of their sensitivity to word order in Japanese. What the researchers found was that learners not only showed sensitivity to the word orders they were exposed to, but many also showed sensitivity to word orders to which they hadn't been exposed, such as *yes/no* questions and simple embedded sentences. In this situation, UG guided the linguistic system to expect that all phrases in Japanese would be complement + head, even though learners had only encountered two kinds of phrases in the experiment and in spite of the fact that their first language, English, was of a different word order. Although we cite one example here, the research within the linguistic theory framework has repeatedly shown how mental representation of language is constrained and guided by UG.

Quick Reflection

Knowing that something like UG constrains acquisition of language, do you think there are implications for the teaching of grammar in textbooks? What are the possible positions a teacher could take on this matter?

General Learning Mechanisms

We learn things all the time that aren't language related. For example, we see a bird we've never seen before, but we know it's a bird. Or we see a symbol (such as the one in Figure 3.1) and know it represents a bird.

Figure 3.1. Graphic Design of a Bird

How is that? From all of the examples of birds we have encountered before, we have extrapolated features to derive something in our minds called "bird features." We learned this from exposure, using what are called *general learning mechanisms* (GLMs). As in the case of talking about UG, we are going to be necessarily brief and perhaps overly simplistic here to avoid the complexities and technical details of how GLMs operate.

In psychology, GLMs are posited to account for much, if not all, human learning. An important component of GLMs is that they tabulate and keep count of the *frequency* of something. In the bird example, the GLMs would have tabulated the frequency with which something identified as a bird had, for example, a beak or feathers. The consistent and frequent appearance of beaks and feathers on many kinds of birds is used by the GLMs to pencil in what is birdlike and what isn't. (There may be other features, to be sure, but we want to keep it simple.)

At the same time, GLMs keep track of the *co-occurrence* of things. In the bird example, beaks and feathers may co-occur and the GLMs set up expectations in the human mind that something with a beak will have feathers and something with feathers will have a beak.

With GLMs, then, all learning is based on what is observable in the environment. General learning mechanisms come into play in language in a number of ways, depending on the theory. On the extreme end, in usage-based approaches, all language acquisition is the result of tabulations, frequency counts, noting co-occurrences, and so on. We will not review the merits of such accounts in this book. Instead, because of our own backgrounds in theoretical linguistics, we take the position that language acquisition involves both UG and GLMs. We saw one example from Japanese (the VanPatten and Smith study mentioned earlier) that demonstrates how UG might operate in one particular instance. How do we see GLMs operating in acquisition?

With GLMs, all learning is based on what is observable in the environment.

Because UG is limited to the formal properties of language (e.g., the syntactic component and its interface with other components), we see GLMs as central to how vocabulary is acquired (and possibly inflections on words), to offer one domain of language. We know from research that there are more frequent words and less frequent words and that people are faster and better at using and recognizing more frequent words than less frequent words. Here is an example. Speakers of English have no problems with the past tense of *drive* or its past participles, *drove* and *driven*. Compared to a verb like *strive*, *drive* is much more frequent in both everyday speech and written language. Because *strive* is much less frequent, English speakers will vacillate between *strove* and *strived* as past tense forms and both are heard: "He strove to do it" and "He strived to do it." In the same vein, speakers will hesitate with the past participle: "I've always strived to do that" and "I've always striven to do that." What happens with GLMs and frequency and tabulations is that we are better at learning the much more frequent things and have more robust representation of those in our heads. We don't learn the less frequent things as well, and those may be represented less robustly—and they may get influenced by the more frequent things! In fact, GLMs are implicated in the U-shaped behavior we saw in Chapter 2.

In a Nutshell ...

General learning mechanisms are posited to account for most of human learning—everything from what things are and what they are called (birds, dogs, flowers, space) to playing bingo. Important in GLMs is the idea that humans unknowingly tabulate things unconsciously, such that frequency and frequency of co-occurrence play important roles in learning.

Take a moment and think about co-occurrence. How would you continue this sentence? What's the first thing that comes to mind? "Pass me the mashed __________, please." Did you say *bananas*? *Peas*? *Yuca*? Try this one: "Would you please shut ________?" Did you say *the door*? *the book in your hand*? *up*? Your first inclinations reflect what is represented in your mind most frequently and most robustly (and perhaps most recently).

In language acquisition, one of the implications of GLMs is that things that are more frequent and have to be learned from exposure are better candidates for (a) being learned sooner and (b) being learned better. Things that are less frequent are learned later and/or not learned as well. Thus, in language acquisition, frequent words and the forms they occur in are learned sooner and better than those that are less frequent. One reason present tense is learned more quickly than something like the future tense in languages is that the present tense is used significantly more frequently in most languages than any kind of future tense. In English, for example, the present tense accounts for about 58% of the verbs anyone hears or reads. The future tense accounts for around 9%. Quite a difference!

> One consequence of GLMs for language acquisition is that frequent words and the forms they occur in are learned sooner and better than those that are less frequent.

Quick Reflection

In most languages, third-person singular is the most frequent verb form in the present tense, for example. What does this mean for you in terms of teaching your language or having concern for other verb forms?

In our view, GLMs are implicated not in the acquisition of syntax and phonology, but instead in the acquisition of vocabulary and word endings (as well as prefixes), to name two examples (e.g., *transport, transportation, transporting, transported*). We also see them implicated in the learning of basic meanings of words and phrases. We saw an example of this with the concept of *bird*. GLMs help us map meaning onto particular words and phrases. Many (but not all) endings on words often link to meaning. For instance, *-s* on the end of a noun in English means "more than one," but *that* in "I know that Russ is intelligent" carries no meaning at all—it is a purely functional means to embed a sentence and is sometimes optional, as in "I know Russ is intelligent." Where we are headed is that GLMs may be implicated in how the pairings of meaning with linguistic device are learned over time. We hinted at this earlier with the example of verb forms. The present tense is acquired before the future tense in part because of its frequency—and this finding implicates GLMs in the acquisition of some, if not many, word endings.

There are some scholars in L2 acquisition who believe GLMs take care of all learning and that there is no such thing as UG working behind the scenes to guide the course of acquisition of the formal components of language. These scholars base their research on psychological constructs rather than linguistic ones, using what are called *usage-based approaches* to acquisition. Clearly, we disagree that GLMs are the only internal ingredient in acquisition, and it is beyond the scope of this book to delve into the UG versus no UG debate. Our own take on the matter is that the debate is often centered on a misunderstanding of UG and what it does, as well as a blurring between the constructs of language and communication. For such matters, we invite the reader to do some research outside of the context of this book. Some of the volumes listed in the readings at the end of this chapter will help you get started. As we see it, there is room for both UG and GLMs, but they may operate on different aspects of language and in different ways during acquisition.

External Ingredients

The concept of external ingredients refers to anything that is not directly related to language or learning mechanisms. In this context, we mean things that aren't related to Universal Grammar or to GLMs. In this section, we will review three of the most important external ingredients discussed in the research: input, interaction, and disposition.

Input

Input is an everyday word. We use it all the time in expressions like "I would like your input on something" or "That plug goes into the input jack on the back of the TV." But in acquisition, *input* has a particular meaning. It refers to language that learners are exposed to in communicative contexts. That is, it is language that learners hear (see) or read for meaning. *Input* does not refer to language that learners practice or manipulate (e.g., "change the present to the past tense"; "repeat after me"). Examples of input include, but are not limited to,

- a story read or listened to for entertainment;
- instructions on what to do (e.g., "Turn to page 32 in your book", "Make a list of five things that make you happy", "Please fill out this form and sign and date it", "Do not take more than eight [8] capsules in a 24-hour period");
- what someone else says during a conversation (e.g., "I was so angry I left." "What do you think?"; "Hey, are you listening to me?");
- items on a questionnaire; and
- listening to a description in order to select an image, draw what was heard, or put a series of images in order, for example.

Not all input is created equal. In L2 research, we often talk about comprehensibility of input. For acquisition to occur, input needs to be communicative (i.e., encode some kind of message or meaning), but it also needs to be comprehensible. After all, if learners can't understand what they hear or read, then it's all just noise. Acquisition, in the simplest of terms, is a byproduct of comprehension. The more learners comprehend language they hear, see, or read, the better the chances are they will get useful data for acquisition. We underscore here that comprehension doesn't *guarantee* acquisition, but it is necessary for acquisition to occur.

Not all input is created equal. In L2 research, we often talk about comprehensibility of input.

Input, then, is something external to the learning devices. What is more, it is something external to learners themselves. Input contains the data that learning devices ultimately need for the creation of a linguistic system. Did you notice we said, "contains the data"? Here, we are hinting at something foreshadowed in Chapter 2—namely, that just because something occurs in the input doesn't mean the learning devices make use of it. Acquisition is highly selective at all stages, and learners' internal devices decide what pieces and parts of input are relevant for acquisition at a given time.

Quick Reflection

If learners' internal devices pick and choose data from communicatively embedded input, does this mean you have to teach things and make learners practice them because they might "miss them" in the input? Or does it mean you should change your expectations about language acquisition?

The bottom line is that input is perhaps the most fundamental external ingredient in language acquisition. Whether you're a child, a teenager, or an adult, access to comprehensible, communicatively embedded input fuels language acquisition. Anything else is secondary, at best, to the role of input. When these ideas were first developed in the late 1970s, they were considered part of a working hypothesis and were even viewed by some as heretical. However, the evidence accumulated since the early days of L2 research overwhelmingly supports the central role of input in acquisition such that in mainstream L2 scholarship, the fundamental role of input is taken as fact. Consider for just a moment what you read in Chapter 2 on ordered development. Clearly, the kind of ordered development we reviewed in that chapter suggests that learners are finding their way through acquisition piecemeal, and the data they use for the piecemeal construction of a system are found in the communicatively embedded input they receive.

In a Nutshell ...

Communicatively embedded input contains the data on which internal mechanisms eventually operate. For the input to be maximally useful, it must be comprehensible (or perhaps maximally comprehensible). Otherwise, input would just be noise. Input is a necessary ingredient in acquisition, but it doesn't guarantee acquisition. *(cont.)*

What do you think makes input comprehensible? How does a 1- or 2-year-old get such input from the environment? Have you ever looked closely at parent-child interactions when the child is barely toddling? What about teenagers and adults learning an L2? How is input made comprehensible?

Interaction

Interaction is a particular facet of communication. Remembering that communication is the expression and interpretation of meaning in a given context for a given purpose, interaction is the process by which communication happens between two or more entities. In L2 research, interaction is almost exclusively examined as a communicative event between two people. During an interaction, people take turns, as in the following example:

Bill: Well, I finally wrote that last section.
Russ: I know. I saw that in the DropBox.
Bill: Have you had time to look at it?
Russ: It's on my schedule for tomorrow.

Interaction is often the most frequent manner in which learners get exposed to comprehensible, communicatively embedded input.

How is interaction relevant as an external ingredient in language acquisition? It is relevant in a number of ways. First, it is often the most frequent way learners get exposed to comprehensible, communicatively embedded input. Unlike when someone is watching a movie or TV, during which a person's attention could drift or the person could stop paying attention altogether (e.g., shut the TV off), interactions directly involve the learner. The learner may have what we call a *higher attention stake* in interactions because the other person is dependent on the learner for the interaction to flow and be successful. As such, the learner pays more attention to what is being said and actively works at comprehension. It's hard for the learner to tune out.

A second way in which interactions are relevant to language acquisition is that they allow for the negotiation of meaning if something is not understood or is misunderstood. Unlike while watching a movie or something similar, during which learners can't stop an actor or speaker and say, "Huh? I didn't get that," interactions do leave space for learners and their interlocutors to actively work at being mutually understood. Here's an example (NS = native speaker; NNS = non-native speaker).

NS: Come on. You can help me fold clothes.
NNS: [puzzled look] fo-fold …
NS: Yeah. Fold clothes.
NNS: [still puzzled look]
NS: Like this. [mimics folding clothes]
NNS: Oh.

In this scenario, there was a problem with comprehension of the last two words of the NS's sentence. The two speakers entered into a phase of negotiation where the NNS signaled non-comprehension twice and then the NS moved to clarify his meaning. In this example, the issue was the non-comprehension of a specific word. Sometimes, however, an entire sentence might be misinterpreted, as in this example:.

NS: John was hit by a car on a side road.
NNS: What? He-he hit a car?
NS: No. No. He was hit by a car.
NNS: [slightly puzzled look]
NS: A car hit him! A car hit John!

In this scenario, the NNS misinterpreted a passive sentence as an active one. The two speakers enter into a brief phase of negotiation of meaning until the NS rephrases his meaning in a different way.

Quick Reflection

Consider how you interact or might interact with learners in the classroom. Are you focused on the expression and interpretation of meaning or on learners "getting the language right"?

According to many scholars working in the field of interaction research, interaction not only provides modified and adjusted input so that comprehension is successful, but such negotiations of meaning may also bring a piece of language into the realm of attention for the learner that may be useful for acquisition. So far, the research is clear how this might work for vocabulary and for certain high-stakes pronunciation issues (e.g., when either a learner's pronunciation interferes with the expression of meaning or when a learner misinterprets someone else's meaning because of non-native processing of speech sounds). However, it is less clear how interaction affects the processes governed by UG and some of the processes involved in GLMs. Our take on the matter is that interaction may assist in an indirect way in the acquisition of those parts of language that map onto meaning critical to sentence comprehension. We gave an example earlier with the active and passive distinction. When learners misinterpret passive sentences as active ones, but the miscomprehension is detected and remedied during some phase of the interaction, learners may begin to pencil in that something about the passive sentence is different. This does not mean they acquire passives on the spot or will do so next time they encounter a passive sentence. What it does suggest is that learners' internal devices may be unconsciously alerted to something about that sentence, which may be the first step in the acquisition of some elements of language.

According to some scholars, negotiation of meaning may bring a piece of language into the realm of attention for the learner that may be useful for acquisition.

In a Nutshell ...

Interaction refers to what happens between people engaged in some kind of conversation. Although we can talk about people "interacting" with a text, for example, in the context of language acquisition we mean interaction related to conversational exchanges. Interaction provides a number of benefits, including (but not limited to) making input more comprehensible and pushing learners to pay attention more (i.e., the input is more "relevant" because learners have a stake in the conversation).

Try to reflect on your earliest days learning a second language. How much did you hear? How difficult was comprehension? Do you still experience comprehension problems? How do those get resolved?

Disposition

Talking about disposition as an external ingredient can be confusing. Disposition refers to such things as attitude, motivation, and perceived self, and these concepts refer to something in the learner's personality. Wouldn't that be internal? The answer is yes, these are learner internal constructs, but they are external to the devices responsible for the development of a mental representation of language. That is, they are independent of and do not directly interact with learning devices, in just the same way that whatever regulates your heartbeat is internal to your body but external to the learning devices for language.

Disposition does not act directly on learning. That is, nothing about a person's attitude or motivation interacts with Universal Grammar's principle that all phrases must have a head and a complement or with the two possible choices for languages (head + complement or complement + head). Learners do not, for example, have a negative or positive attitude toward phrase structure, the Extended Project Principle, features such as Tense, or the operation Move. They don't even know these things exist! The same is true for something like motivation. Learners are not motivated or unmotivated to learn something like *wh-* movement in English and Spanish or complement + head in Japanese. Again, these are concepts with which the learner is unfamiliar, so it is impossible for their acquisition to be linked directly to motivation.

Yet disposition as an external ingredient does have a significant role to play in acquisition, and that role is related to learners' access to—guess what—input and interaction. Learners with a positive attitude, high levels of motivation, healthy self-perceptions, and other traits may be more inclined to seek out input and interaction during acquisition. They are more likely to read in the L2. They are more likely to consider traveling to and perhaps living in another country where the language is spoken. They are more likely to stick with the long haul needed for acquisition. What this means, then, is that such learners get more input, probably better-quality input through interaction, and simply more time with the language. The internal devices need lots of input over time because the process of building a linguistic system in the mind is slow. In Chapter 2, we saw how development is ordered over time and that there is staged development in the acquisition of particular parts of language. Learners may take a long time—even years—to traverse all the stages in the acquisition of all facets of language. What propels acquisition along, then, is access to appropriate input, and what encourages access is the learner's disposition. Learners have to want to acquire language enough to stick with it, and wanting or desire is inextricably entangled with a learner's disposition.

Disposition as an external ingredient has a significant role to play in acquisition related to learner access to input and interaction.

Quick Reflection

What is the teacher's role in learners' disposition and motivation in the classroom? What about the teacher's own disposition and motivation?

Disposition is what researchers call a type of *individual difference*. That is, as individuals, we vary in our dispositions. To be sure, there are other individual differences that researchers examine. We would also classify them as external to the learning devices. These include, for instance, language aptitude and working memory. It is not our intent to review all individual differences in this book, as there are whole books on these topics. But for the purpose of this chapter, we point out several issues related to such individual differences.

While disposition is psychosocial in nature and clearly tied to access to input and interaction, differences such as language aptitude and working memory are tied to cognition. As such, there have been attempts to link these differences directly to acquisition in some way. However, the results have not been successful. Language aptitude has been shown to be a predictor or correlate of explicit learning, but as we will see in the next chapter, language acquisition is largely implicit in nature. This means acquisition happens to learners without them being aware of the processes or the representation that evolves over time. For example, language aptitude is a predictor of how well learners do on certain kinds of tests of surface features of language that learners can and do practice explicitly or can learn explicitly (e.g., verb forms, words, rules of thumb). However, aptitude is not a predictor of, say, stages of acquisition and ordered development (as seen in Chapter 2) or of whether learners project complement + head structure onto Japanese after only 100 sentences (as examined in the VanPatten and Smith study). In another 2013 study involving Spanish, French, German, and Russian, VanPatten and his colleagues demonstrated that aptitude is not related to how and when learners begin to correctly process sentences of various words orders (e.g., subject-verb-object and object-verb-subject). So, aptitude may be relevant to some classroom teachers who are more oriented to explicit learning and explicit outcomes, but it is not relevant to researchers interested in how mental representation develops over time or to teachers who take a more acquisition-oriented approach to classrooms.

Scholars such as Gisela Granena have recently begun to examine what is called *implicit language aptitude*. What Granena argues is that unlike traditional concepts of language aptitude tied to explicit learning, there is a kind of aptitude related to implicit learning, and this aptitude may account for acquisitional differences such as how fast learners acquire language and how far they get compared with other learners. We will examine the role of implicit learning in Chapter 4 but wanted to mention implicit aptitude here as an alternative to the more traditional understanding of language aptitude that emerged in the 1950s.

A different kind of individual difference, *working memory* refers to the ability of listeners and readers to hold bits of information during real-time, millisecond-by-millisecond comprehension. People are said to vary on a limited scale of working memory ability, and the general idea is that people with higher working memory capacity comprehend more and comprehend information faster than those with lower working memory capacity. This, at least, is the claim in research on L1 reading (and listening). The research on the relationship to L2 acquisition is less clear. In fact, a complete review of the literature in this regard would show that there is no clear evidence that working memory affects acquisition in any significant way. This seems counterintuitive when one considers that acquisition is a byproduct of comprehension. Would those who comprehend more and comprehend it better be faster at acquisition? Theoretically, yes, but the research just hasn't provided satisfactory evidence to date. In any event, working memory exists external to the learning devices because, as in the case of disposition and aptitude, there is nothing about working memory that directly affects how UG guides acquisition, although it may interact to a certain extent with general learning mechanisms (e.g., the ability to hold a lexical item in working memory while trying to figure out what it means). To be sure, there is some suggestive research relating working memory and communicative ability (e.g., planning what you're going to say, negotiated interactions), but there's no research that actually speaks to how mental representation for language evolves over time as a result of the effects of working memory.

Quick Reflection

How concerned are you about individual differences? Do they affect what you think about acquisition and how you teach?

Did you know that individual differences in rate of learning are evident in child L1 acquisition as well? That is, if you take 100 children at the age of 2 years old all acquiring language in the same environment, you will see some that are further along in acquisition than others. Researchers in child L1 acquisition have looked at a number of factors to determine the source of individual variation in children's language acquisition. However, to date, there is no consensus concerning why differences in rate of acquisition appear in children except in one case: the role of quantity and quality of input. There is considerable research showing that variations in the linguistic environment affect the rate of child L1 acquisition. Given that there are individual differences in child L1 acquisition, no matter the source, it's not surprising to find the same in L2 acquisition.

In a Nutshell ...

Disposition refers to aspects of a learner's personality such as attitude, motivation, and self-perception. While internal to the learner, these constructs exist outside the learning mechanisms—hence their designation as external. Other non-learning mechanisms include working memory and aptitude. None of these constructs interact directly with the learning mechanisms, but the ones related to disposition may have a significant impact on the extent to which learners seek out input and interaction with others.

Think about people who have gone on to be advanced speakers and knowers of another language. They didn't limit themselves to classrooms and textbooks. What else did they do, and can you relate that to what you perceive to be their dispositions?

Summary

In this chapter, we have reviewed the basic ingredients that are internal and external to the creation of a linguistic system, as described in Chapter 1. Internal ingredients are those that make up the learning devices: Universal Grammar and general learning mechanisms (GLMs). Both are seen to be at work in shaping a learner's evolving mental representation of language, but they do not act in the same way and do not operate on the same aspects of language. These are the ingredients responsible for what gets processed from the environment and how that information is incorporated into the evolving system along with any consequences for its incorporation.

The external ingredients are those that fall outside of the learning devices—such as disposition (e.g., attitude, motivation, self-perception), language aptitude, and working memory—as well as those that fall outside of learners themselves—namely, input and interaction. Input is seen as a central and necessary ingredient, with interaction playing a secondary role in the way it may aid in optimizing the comprehensibility of input and perhaps bringing some things to learners' unconscious attention (e.g., the active/passive example we shared). Disposition is related to access to input and interaction, but it is unclear just what working memory contributes to L2 acquisition in terms of how the mental representation evolves over time. Language aptitude is viewed as largely unrelated to acquisition. The reason for this may become clearer in the next chapter when we review the idea that implicit rather than explicit learning is central to acquisition.

Before concluding, we want to remind the reader that the title of this chapter is "Basic Ingredients." We want to emphasize the word *basic*. What is presented here really are the bare bones of ingredients—and they are presented in the most basic of ways. Language acquisition is a complex phenomenon. Myriad things both internal and external work simultaneously such that no single thing can be pulled out as the most important part of acquisition. Ultimately, all factors are important in one way or another. In this chapter, we have attempted to focus your attention on a few to get you thinking about just how marvelous language acquisition must be given that it involves so many moving parts.

As a reader, you may have kept in mind Chapters 1 and 2 while contemplating the contents of this chapter. If you did, the major points of this chapter may not be surprising, even without a thorough review of all relevant research that you might find in one of the many thick books on language acquisition. Because we are clear on what we mean language to be and we are sure of ordered development and what it suggests, the division between internal and external ingredients along with what they do in acquisition makes sense to us, as it does to many scholars. We hope it makes sense to you.

Selected References and Suggested Readings

Two chapters from a recent publication will augment the information on internal ingredients:

Ellis, N., & Wulff, S. (2020). Usage-based approaches to L2 acquisition. In B. VanPatten, G. D. Keating, & S. Wulff (Eds.), *Theories in second language acquisition* (pp. 63–82). Routledge.

White, L. (2020). Linguistic theory, Universal Grammar, and second language acquisition. In B. VanPatten, G. D. Keating, & S. Wulff (Eds.), *Theories in second language acquisition* (pp. 19–39). Routledge.

In addition, we refer you to the volume edited by Julia Herschensohn and Martha Young-Scholten in which Parts II and III are titled, respectively, "Internal Ingredients" and "External Ingredients."

Herschensohn, J., & Young-Scholten, M. (Eds.). (2013). *The Cambridge handbook of second language acquisition*. Cambridge University Press.

Here are sources for the VanPatten and Smith study, as well as the study on Spanish, German, French, and Russian mentioned in this chapter:

VanPatten, B., Borst, S., Collopy, E., Qualin, A., & Price, J. (2013). Explicit information, grammatical sensitivity, and the First-noun Principle: A cross-linguistic study in processing instruction. *The Modern Language Journal, 92,* 506–527.

VanPatten, B., & Smith, M. (2015). Aptitude as grammatical sensitivity and the initial stages of learning Japanese as an L2: Parametric variation and case marking. *Studies in Second Language Acquisition, 37*, 135–165.

The following book provides good overview chapters on topics such as language aptitude, motivation, identity, and working memory:

Gass, S. M., & Mackey, A. (2012). *The Routledge handbook of second language acquisition*. Routledge.

In addition, the following book discusses newer developments in implicit language aptitude:

Granena, G. (2020). *Implicit language aptitude.* Cambridge University Press.

For a dated but still relevant overview of input and interaction, we recommend the following chapter:

Gass, S. M. (2003). Input and interaction. In C. J. Doughty & Long (Eds.), *The handbook of second language acquisition* (pp. 224–255). Blackwell.

If you are inclined to read about individual differences in children's L1 acquisition, we suggest this overview article:

Kidd, E., & Donnelly, S. (2020). Individual differences in first language acquisition. *Annual Review of Linguistics, 6,* 319–340.

Thinking Some More

1. Return to the "Before You Read" box at the beginning of this chapter. What do you think of the statements now? Have you changed your mind about anything?
2. Based on what you read about Universal Grammar, which of the following metaphors best captures what it does? (You can opt for more than one, but you need to explain your options.)
   - It's similar to the Constitution of the United States: It contains basic laws and principles that all states must adhere to, but not all states are alike in their laws.
   - It's like human DNA: It governs the basic properties of human bodies, but not all human bodies look exactly alike.
   - It's akin to cultural norms: There are cultural norms that all cultures seem to follow, but not all cultures are exactly alike.
   - It's reminiscent of laundry detergents: They all have the same basic cleaning ingredients and only vary in superficial ways.
3. General learning mechanisms (GLMs) are reputed to be involved in all of human learning, regardless of the focus of learning, age, or context. This idea suggests that learning unrelated skills such as playing the piano, reading, dancing, and speaking a language share the same mechanisms. In this chapter, we have outlined one area in which GLMs may play a role related to languages: the learning of vocabulary words and their meanings. How do you see the learning of vocabulary words and meanings involving the same mechanisms as, say, learning to play the piano or learning to read? (Keep in mind the fundamental role of frequency and co-occurring items in the environment as you ponder this question.)
4. After reading about disposition, how can you best express its role in language acquisition? Which of the following statements makes the most sense to you based on what you've read in this chapter?
   - Disposition shapes the course and path of development, but it does not affect how far learners get in acquiring another language.

- Disposition affects how far learners get in acquiring another language, but it does not affect the course and path of development.
- Disposition affects all aspects of language acquisition.

5. Research conducted in the 1950s and early 1960s compared learners who studied abroad and those who did not. The research provided evidence that those who studied abroad for a full year and lived with a family were the most likely to reach Advanced and higher levels on the ACTFL Proficiency Scale. Those who studied abroad for only 1 semester were significantly less likely to make it to the Advanced level, and those who did not study abroad rarely if ever made it to the Advanced level. Assuming that some kind of mental representation underlies what Advanced learners can do with language in communication, what does this research suggest about input and interaction and their roles in acquisition?

   Contemporary research on study abroad does not reveal the same strong patterns of level attainment. That is, fewer learners reach the Advanced level when studying abroad. What is different about L2 environments and learners today compared with the 1950s? List as many ideas as you can.

6. Interaction has been shown to help make input comprehensible and more relevant to learners. The bulk of the research has been done on face-to-face interactions. Do you think chatting online can accomplish the same outcomes? Can it replace face-to-face interactions? Why or why not? What about video chats and interactions?

7. List five or six takeaway ideas from this chapter. What would you like to share with colleagues who have not read this chapter and may be unfamiliar with the topic?

Considering the Classroom

1. If both UG and GLMs guide and constrain acquisition, what do you think is the role of explicitly teaching features such as grammar and vocabulary? Are there any clear implications? Keep in mind what you have read in the previous chapters as well. Here are some statements you might consider:

- Teaching grammar might be not be so useful, but working explicitly with vocabulary seems useful.
- Teaching vocabulary might not be so useful, but working explicitly with grammar seems warranted.
- Teaching both grammar and vocabulary explicitly seems warranted.
- Neither grammar nor vocabulary needs to be taught explicitly.

2. If comprehensible and communicatively embedded input is an essential ingredient for language acquisition, what implications are there for the classroom? Note that ACTFL recommends that 90% of class time be conducted in the language. How do you interpret that statement based on what you understand about the role of input in language acquisition?
3. Interaction is an external ingredient in acquisition. Learners who interact are clearly more engaged and paying attention. Many teachers puzzle over what interaction means when it comes to beginning learners: How can they interact when they don't have language? The question, then, is this: Does interaction always mean speaking, especially speaking in sentences? What other ways can learners be actively involved with a teacher's communicative input without speaking or speaking in sentences? How do children interact with others when they are 2 years old when their language is "limited"?
4. Do a search on YouTube for TPRS, which stands for Teaching Proficiency through Reading and Storytelling. How are learners interacting in those classes? What do the teachers seem to expect and accept as student interactions?
5. Individual differences in acquisition play out in terms of both rate of acquisition and how far learners get. A class of 30 students, for instance, could display variations in what learners can do with language (and how language is unfolding in their heads). Do you think grading students using traditional notions such as letter grades or percentages is fair? Do students have control over their individual differences? If not, what alternatives to traditional testing and entering grades in a book might teachers consider? Read the following articles for more on this topic:

VanPatten, B., & Hopkins, W. P. (2015). Can-do statements for a basic language program. *CLEAR News*, *19*, 1–5.

VanPatten, B., Trego, D., & Hopkins, W. P. (2015). In-class versus online testing in university-level language courses: A research report. *Foreign Language Annals*, *48*, 659–668.

FAQs

If you'd like, go to Chapter 5, "Frequently Asked Questions," and check out the questions that are related to topics in this chapter. (The numbers match the numbers for the questions in Chapter 5.)

7. But isn't L2 acquisition different from L1 acquisition?
8. Don't learners have to speak to learn a language?
9. Doesn't everything come down to motivation?
10. What about individual differences and different learning styles?

4

Chapter 4

The Centrality of Implicit Learning

Students may spend a good deal of time trying to learn material explicitly. When it comes to language acquisition, however, it is increasingly clear that implicit learning plays the primary role.

Before You Read

Consider these statements, then come back after reading this chapter to see if your thoughts have changed.

- Certain aspects of a second language must be learned explicitly.
- A sign of successful acquisition is that learners can figure out and state the "rules" of a language on their own.
- Learning a word basically means learning its meaning.
- Learning a language is different from learning about other topics, such as biology.

Have you ever stopped to think how you got all of the knowledge that you have in your head? Have you ever stopped to think of how that knowledge is stored, what it actually looks like in your mind? For example, how did you learn the meaning of *word*? Did someone teach you what a word was? And what do you think is in your head when it comes to the word *word*? If you're like most people, you really don't know how this word got in your head or what its representation looks like.

In Chapters 1 and 3, we saw how speakers come to know things about their first language without being consciously aware of them (e.g., "redecorate a room" is fine but "*restep in the puddle" is not). People know what sounds good and what sounds bad, and this often does not line up with the prescriptive rules taught in school. In this chapter, we will explore this concept and related matters as we delve into an ever-increasing understanding among scholars: that implicit learning and the development of an implicit mental representation of language are central to acquisition of both L1 and L2. We want to acknowledge the influence that a recent publication by Bill VanPatten and Megan Smith has had on the content of this chapter (the full reference is included at the end of this chapter). To begin, we will look at some definitions using the words *explicit* and *implicit*.

Some Definitions

Our first definitions center on the terms *explicit knowledge* and *implicit knowledge*. Explicit knowledge refers to knowledge people possess that they can verbalize (or think they can verbalize). For example, people can verbalize what a letter is: It is written communication you receive in the mail. Whether or not this is an accurate verbalization or is complete in defining what a letter is, people can articulate something about what a letter is. Implicit knowledge refers to knowledge that people have a great deal of difficulty verbalizing or can't verbalize at all. For example, in contrast to a letter, people have extreme difficulty verbalizing what a word is. They know one when they see one, but articulating just what constitutes a word generally escapes the average person. They wind up going down a rabbit hole, relying on equally abstract concepts to try to articulate what a word is. You may recall from Chapter 1 that people have difficulty stating what a verb is. Whatever they say, they tend to get it wrong. Yet people use verbs all the time and know one when they hear it or see it.

Two other terms are *explicit learning* and *implicit learning*. Learning in and of itself basically means creating or altering cognitive structures or behaviors based on some kind of stimulus from the environment. Explicit learning means creating such structures or behaviors by using conscious processes and doing so generally, but not always, with intention. Generally, you are aware of what you are learning. Implicit learning means constructing new cognitive structures or behaviors without conscious processes and almost always without intention. You are generally not aware of what you are learning.

We want to note a few things before moving on. First, all researchers agree that learners must arrive at some kind of implicit knowledge of language. However, what researchers in second language acquisition (SLA) tend not to do when discussing explicit and implicit learning is define just what that knowledge is. You will notice that we consistently use *implicit mental representation* in this chapter when talking about language, not *implicit knowledge*. This is purposeful. We do not want to lead anyone to think that the implicit representation we have in our heads for language in any way resembles explicit knowledge. We will touch on this issue at various times in this chapter. Second, in L2 research, explicit learning is often conflated with explicit teaching and instruction. Although teaching often involves explicit learning, explicit learning in and of itself doesn't have to be done in a classroom. The ultimate issue, then, is not what teachers do, but what learners do—that is, the focus should be on the processes in which learners engage when confronted with linguistic data. You will recall from Chapter 3 that communicatively embedded input is a necessary external ingredient in acquisition. So, the real question that confronts us is this: Do learners engage explicit or implicit learning when confronted with data in the input? Still, because of the field of SLA, we will touch on the role of explicit teaching in this chapter.

All researchers agree that learners must arrive at some kind of implicit knowledge of language.

This fundamental question is traceable to foundational research by Andrew Reber, a psychologist whose research strongly points to implicit learning of non-linguistic patterns. In Reber's research, which began in the 1960s, people were exposed to strings of letters generated by a set of underlying "rules." They might have seen, for example, strings such as MV, MSV, MSSV, MSVS, VXV, VX, and VXV. After people were exposed to these strings of letters, Reber would test them on novel strings of letters they hadn't seen to determine if they could identify which strings were good and which ones weren't. In other words, he was testing to see if his participants had somehow learned the underlying "rules." What he found over the years was that participants could make determinations about good and bad strings they hadn't been exposed to, but they couldn't articulate why they had made these determinations. This was true even when he asked them specifically to pay attention and try to figure out the rules. Reber concluded that learning such patterns was implicit in nature and resulted in implicit knowledge. Of course, strings of letters aren't language, and language doesn't consist of patterns, but Reber's work is suggestive of how the mind works.

Quick Reflection

Do you use the word *patterns* when teaching or interacting with colleagues? What do you think this word signals to learners (or others) about language?

It is accepted in scholarship that L1 acquisition involves largely implicit learning and processes. What about L2 acquisition? The possible centrality of implicit learning in L2 research dates back to the 1970s and is most widely attributed to Stephen Krashen. He couched explicit and implicit learning in terms of learning and acquisition, respectively. His claim was that acquisition (involving implicit processes), rather than learning, was central to successful L2 development. Because acquisition was input dependent (see Chapter 3), learning from input was largely, if not exclusively, implicit in nature.

Before we examine any research supporting such claims, let's remind ourselves of something important—the nature of language. From that discussion, we will posit why a theory of language points to the centrality of implicit learning.

Language (Again)

In this section, we return to a fundamental issue in Chapter 1: that language isn't what is found in textbooks. As we discussed in that chapter, language is mental representation. Here, we note two of the basic characteristics of language:

- Language is abstract. This means that language can't be described easily in everyday terms. It does not consist of the concrete rules and charts provided in almost all world language textbooks. Such rules and charts are not psychologically real.
- Language is complex. With this statement, we return to the idea that language consists of a number of different things that interact in ways to create even the simplest of sentences. Even within a single component of language, there is complexity.

Understanding the abstract and complex nature of language leads to the conclusion that it would be extremely difficult—if not impossible—for learning to be largely explicit in nature. Why would we say this? Let's illustrate with a simple sentence in Spanish. As you work through this and aren't a teacher of Spanish, try to imagine the implications for the same sentence in the language you teach. Here's the sentence: *¿Dónde viven tus padres?* 'Where do your parents live?' During learning (i.e., getting data from the input), learners must process words. This leads to an important question: What's in a word? What do learners have to process and store with the word *viven*, for example? Here's a minimal list of what this word contains:

- [meaning: something about living]
- [the sequence of sounds]
- [-N], [+V]: The word is a verb and not a noun or something else.
- [3rd]: The reference is to third person.
- [+plural]: The reference is to more than one entity.
- [+ present, -past]: The time frame is the present.

Even the simple word, *tus*, involves a list of items that need to be encoded:

- [meaning: something about possession]
- [the sequence of sounds]
- [+D]: It has determiner features (not noun features or verb features, for example)
- [+2nd]: The reference is to the other interlocutor.
- [+plural]: The reference is to more than one entity.

In addition to processing all of the features of these two simple words, learners also have to interpret syntactic information when hearing the sentence *Dónde viven tus padres?* First, they have to interpret that it's an interrogative sentence. This, in turn, causes the internal mechanisms to make unconscious note of a word order that is different from declarative sentences (e.g., *Tus padres viven en Chicago.* 'Your parents live in Chicago.'). This then triggers the mechanisms to posit movement of question words, verbs, and other components (see Chapters 1 and 2). So, learners not only process the internal elements of words but also process syntactic information in order to move toward a mental representation of the L2. How can the processing of these abstract properties happen explicitly? Clearly, it doesn't. Why? Because learners' comprehension (and thus their processing of data from the input) would come to a halt if they had to explicitly focus on these items constantly and consistently for every sentence they hear or read.

We (Russ and Bill) take a linguistic perspective on the nature of language, pulling from a particular perspective. Not everyone takes the same perspective. However, even those who do not (e.g., constructionists and other usage-based researchers) tend to concur that implicit learning and processing are central to acquisition. We have provided readings at the end of this chapter that will point you in that direction.

We've just examined one theoretical argument for the centrality of implicit learning in L2 acquisition. But there must be empirical evidence, right? And there is. We'll begin with evidence we've had since the 1970s, which is the focus of the next section.

In a Nutshell ...

Not only is language structure abstract and complex, but what is contained in a word is even abstract and complex.

Ask some friends to tell you everything they can about the word *circle*. What do they come up with? How technical do they get? Do they mention anything about its formal properties? Do they get caught up trying to accurately say what a circle is? Do they have to rely on other concepts to try to define it (e.g., "it's not a square")?

What Ordered Development Tells Us

Remember ordered development from Chapter 2? Ordered development is one of the biggest clues to the centrality of implicit processing in L2 acquisition, but it has been overlooked by many scholars concerned with the explicit and implicit learning issue. Let's see what we mean by looking at an example from Spanish.

If you review Chapter 2, you will remember the first stage in the acquisition of *ser* and *estar* is one in which learners tend to omit these linking verbs, as in **Sara alta* instead of **Sara es alta* ('Sara is tall.') and **Terry no aquí* instead of *Terry no está aquí* ('Terry isn't here'). Why would L1 English speakers omit linking verbs in L2 Spanish when these verbs are required in their L1 and are present in the input in the L2? As a reminder, linking verbs have no inherent meaning, unlike the verbs *eat*, *run,* and *read*. Instead, linking verbs have a purely grammatical function: to carry information regarding tense and person-number. In the first stage in the acquisition of *ser* and *estar*, when these verbs are absent, we have an indication that learners are creating sentences without tense.

At the same time, we know that novice Spanish learners also use bare verbs, which are devoid of tense and person-number indications. For example, learners tend to use one singular verb form such as *come* 'eat' and *toma* 'take/drink,' as opposed to changing the verb endings to indicate tense and person-number (e.g., they will say **yo come* instead of *yo como* 'I eat'). While English doesn't normally mark verbs for person-number, Tense as a feature does exist in English. Still, learners with L1 English don't normally indicate Tense on verbs in the earliest stages of acquiring Spanish.

So, what we have from the *ser/estar* research as well as the research on regular verbs is that learners of Spanish seem to create a mental representation for Spanish early on that is tenseless. In linguistic jargon, they haven't selected Tense as a feature. This is puzzling. First, Tense exists in the L1 for learners of English, but they don't seem to be transferring this feature. Second, Tense as a feature is abundant in the Spanish input to which the learners are exposed. Any complete sentence in Spanish will have indications for Tense on verbs. Third, and perhaps most important for the present discussion, *ser/estar* and verb forms are taught, practiced, and learned explicitly from the very first days of learning Spanish in a classroom. Why, then, would learners create a tenseless system with linking verbs absent and with bare verbs used as a default? As most scholars would see it, learners are implicitly creating a representation for language. They are unaware of what they are doing.

Let's look at one other example. Learners of Russian are taught and practice case endings explicitly. Yet, the research is clear that nominative case is acquired much earlier than instrumental or locative case. Most likely, nominative case is the default case—much like bare verbs in Spanish, as discussed. Thus, learners begin the acquisition of Russian with the idea that there is no case; they slowly pencil in the actual endings over time. If learners are taught case from the beginning, why do they create a system in which case is absent? Our conclusion is that like much of language, the system evolves over time as bits and pieces of data in the input get processed by the internal mechanisms. This process is largely implicit.

Quick Reflection

As a teacher, have you stopped to think about what must be going on in learners' minds as they process and organize language? If you have, what did you think about, and how did this influence your teaching, if at all?

We could offer other examples from ordered development but prefer not to belabor the point. What the examples all point to is that in ordered development, learners are giving us clear clues that they are processing, organizing, and storing linguistic data in an implicit way. Whatever explicit teaching and explicit learning is a part of their experience, it seems not to be central to how language develops in their minds.

A Note About Explicit Learning and Ordered Development

Is ordered development affected by explicit learning and instruction? The answer is no, and the research on this topic dates back to the 1970s and 1980s. A number of scholars—including John Schumann, Patsy Lightbown, Rod Ellis, Maria Pavesi, Teresa Pica, and Manfred Pienemann—have researched this question. In all cases, ordered development is unaffected by either learners' attempts to explicitly learn something or by teachers' attempts to instruct something. Let's return to our two examples from earlier. The two Spanish verbs of "being," *ser* and *estar*, develop in a stagelike way. First, L2 learners omit these verbs, then they begin to acquire *ser*, then *estar*. This seems to be the pattern regardless of the first language of L2 Spanish learners, whether Korean, Chinese, or English. Ordered development also appears in the development

Ordered development is unaffected by learner attempts to explicitly learn something or by teachers' attempts to instruct something.

of Russian case, regardless of instruction. Both L1 and L2 learners acquire nominative case before accusative (in other words, they can talk about subjects before objects). Ordered development is such a strong aspect of acquisition that teachers cannot make their learners acquire *estar* before *ser*, or accusative case before nominative. To be sure, a teacher could explicitly teach the differences between *ser* and *estar* or Russian case endings, subsequently give his or her students a traditional test, and claim that all concepts were "mastered" if everyone earns a perfect score. However, traditional tests are not indicative of underlying mental representation. We will address the question of whether explicit knowledge can turn into implicit mental representation later.

Before moving on, it is important to note the following. A good deal of research on ordered development involves classroom learners who receive explicit instruction and go about the task of explicit learning. Their ordered development resembles the development of learners who don't go about explicit learning or receive instruction.

In a Nutshell ...

Ordered development offers a clear indication that learners are processing and organizing language outside of their awareness. It is also clear that they do so independently of explicit teaching and learning.

Examine the prefaces of several textbooks. Do they make any reference to research on language acquisition as presented here? Do they make mention of ordered development? Consider this question: Why would it be almost impossible to organize language teaching materials around established developmental orders and stages?

Learners "Know" Things They Couldn't Have Learned

There is a phenomenon in both L1 and L2 acquisition called the Poverty of the Stimulus situation, or POS for short. What the POS situation refers to is having implicit representation for language even when it seems impossible to have developed this representation based on clues from the environment. Although many of us like to think that communicatively embedded input contains everything about language we can see, sometimes it doesn't.

We can illustrate with an example we've used elsewhere in this book.

Every L1 and L2 learner of English is confronted with contractions in the language they are exposed to. They hear *I've, should've, wanna, gonna,* and others. So, it's not difficult for either an L1 or L2 learner to arrive at a mental representation for English that says, "Contractions are allowed in this language." The problem arises when we try to figure out why such speakers also know when contractions aren't allowed. We can compare the sentences below to see what we mean.

(1) I have done it./I've done it./Should I have done it?/*Should I've done it?

(2) Who do you want to tell?/Who do you wanna tell?/Who do you want to tell Bob?/*Who do you wanna tell Bob?

(3) Bill's going to do it./Bill's gonna do it./Bill's going to the store./*Bill's gonna the store.

What the sentences illustrate is that contractions are allowed in some contexts but not in others. L1 and L2 learners of English are typically only exposed to contexts in which contractions are allowed, yet their representations for contractions also include when contractions are prohibited. They don't get this information from the input, and they aren't taught this information, either. So, how do they "know" when contractions aren't allowed?

Here's a tougher example that will take some time to work through. Languages like Spanish, Italian, Turkish, and Japanese all permit null subjects. Thus, in Spanish, for example, both answers to the question are grammatical, although (b) sounds odd.

(4) ¿Dónde está Russ? 'Where's Russ?'
  a. Está en casa.
  b. Él está en casa. 'He's at home.'

The answer in (a) contains a null subject pronoun (one we can't see or hear), while the answer in (b) contains an overt subject pronoun (one we can see or hear). Evidence for null and overt subject pronouns is readily evident in the input learners are exposed to, and the distinction between the two types of pronouns is an accepted fact in linguistic circles. Now let's take the following sentences:

(5) Nadie admite que es responsable/que él es responsable.
'Nobody admits he's responsible.'

(6) ¿Quién admite que es responsable/que él es responsable?
'Who admits he's responsible?'

In both (5) and (6), the null subject pronoun can refer to "nobody" or to "who," or it can refer to some third entity (e.g., maybe they're talking about a politician, lawyer, or train conductor). However, in neither case can the overt subject *él* refer to "nobody" or "who." There seems to be a constraint on what overt subject pronouns can refer to in languages like Spanish, Italian, Turkish, and Japanese. This constraint is not evident in the input, and no L1 or L2 speaker of these languages is taught this constraint. Learners simply (unconsciously) know it exists. We note that English and German don't have such a constraint because these languages don't allow null subjects in the same way our sample languages do.

Quick Reflection

Whether you teach a language that allows null subject pronouns or one that doesn't, how much do you worry about learners "getting" how pronouns work? How much did you worry about it when learning another language?

Note that in POS situations, we can't simply conclude that because something doesn't appear in the input, it must be disallowed. If that were the case, we could only produce what we've heard. We could never create new sentences or combine them in new ways because, well, we've never encountered them in the input. What is more, there is research that shows that speakers (both L1 and L2) accept grammatical sentences as fine for structures they haven't encountered yet. So, absence in the input doesn't mean prohibited. Just because we haven't heard it doesn't mean we can't do it. People, then, come to have a mental representation for language that they weren't exposed to and didn't learn in any explicit manner.

These POS situations and the implicit mental representation that people possess about such constraints and prohibitions demonstrate that learners in all contexts arrive at something about language without any kind of awareness. In other words, these constraints aren't learned explicitly. There is substantial research on the POS situation in L2 contexts (as there is in L1), and this research provides one more kind of evidence regarding the centrality of implicit learning and processes in L2 acquisition.

POS situations demonstrate that learners in all contexts arrive at something about language without any kind of awareness.

There are some scholars, such as Adele Goldberg, who believe many documented POS situations can be learned from the input. As with other topics we've discussed in this book, these researchers would argue that the mental representation is acquired implicitly, even if the characterization of that knowledge is different from what other approaches might assert.

In a Nutshell ...

People come to have unconscious knowledge about language that they can't have learned from the input. Something internal and involving implicit processes must be at work in acquisition for this to happen.

Try this exercise with some friends. Ask them if this is a good sentence and why or why not: "The woman are a nice lady." After they give their answer, ask them about this sentence: "I wonder what he thinks who has done." Do their responses differ with the two examples? Can they explain one but not the other or identify the problem in one but not the other? [Note for yourself: "I wonder who he thinks has done what" is fine, so the question is why the "who" can move but not the "what" and how anyone even knows this.]

Laboratory Research on Explicit and Implicit Instruction

One of the most researched areas involving explicit and implicit learning is about the effect that instruction has on acquisition. We noted earlier that ordered development is not altered by instruction. In this section, we will look at the following related issues in laboratory-based studies:

- explicit versus implicit instruction
- long-term effects of instruction
- when instruction has a negative effect

Explicit Versus Implicit Instruction

In this line of research, scholars typically compare three groups of learners: one that receives explicit instruction, one that receives implicit instruction, and one that receives no instruction (we will define each in a moment). Prior to instruction, learners are given a pretest of knowledge on a particular structure (e.g., past-tense endings), and after instruction learners are given a posttest. The posttest scores are compared to the pretest scores. If the posttest scores are significantly higher (determined by statistical analysis), the scholar may claim that acquisition was affected and instruction made a difference.

Of relevance here is the difference between explicit instruction and implicit instruction. Explicit instruction refers to giving learners rules or information about the language (usually those found in textbooks and online sources), then having them practice in some way or interact with some kind of input. Implicit instruction also involves practicing or interacting with input, but there is no provision of rules or information about the language, even though such rules and information are the object of instruction. Two meta-analyses of all the qualifying research were published in 2010 and 2015. A meta-analysis reviews research studies to date, and a particular statistical analysis is done on all of the results to see if there is an overall effect across the studies. The conclusion of both meta-analyses was that both explicit and implicit instructional groups tended to make gains from pretest to posttest, but the learners in the explicit groups tended to do better. Many scholars have taken these results to mean that explicit learning is involved in acquisition. However, three caveats are in order.

First, the difference between explicit and implicit instruction is illusory. When learners come into a laboratory study, the researchers cannot turn off the learners' training as explicit learners of textbook rules. That is, the participants are likely acting like classroom learners and trying to explicitly learn the rules even when they are in the implicit instruction group. They have been trained to approach language this way. And in classrooms, when teachers attempt to engage in implicit teaching, they are still trying to actively induce rules, verb forms, case endings, and so on in their learners. If learners consciously pick up on what patterns or rules the teacher is trying to induce, they are no longer learning implicitly, by definition. So, the research on explicit and implicit teaching tells us very little about the difference between explicit and implicit *learning*. Although explicit teaching is assumed to result in explicit learning and implicit teaching is assumed to result in implicit learning, we cannot necessarily conclude that this is the case.

The difference between explicit and implicit instruction is illusory.

A second caveat is that the method of testing learners' knowledge is biased. To elaborate, when researchers attempt to compare explicit and implicit instruction, they often use tests that are better at detecting explicit knowledge than implicit mental representation. This caveat was first noted in a 2000 publication by John Norris and Lourdes Ortega, who conducted a meta-analysis of research on the effects of instruction. In their discussion, Norris and Ortega cautioned the reader that well over 90% of the studies used tests that were biased for explicit knowledge, so it would be expected that a positive effect of explicit teaching would show up in the results. This cautionary note generally goes unheeded by researchers looking at the effects of instruction.

The bias for explicit knowledge is likely related to the use of textbook rules and surface features of language. These kinds of grammatical items are tailor made for explicit learning. Whether or not researchers take a principled approach to the nature of language (see Chapter 1), they do like textbook-type rules because they are easily codable and teachable for research.

But as we have said repeatedly in this book, textbook rules aren't what winds up in our heads. Mental representation for language is qualitatively different from such rules. A recent study that takes a theoretical perspective on language was conducted by Mien-Jen Wu and Tania Ionin, who tried to explicitly teach an abstract and complex feature of language called "inverse scope." Their results show that implicit mental representation is not affected by explicit teaching and learning.

A third caveat in this kind of research involves the inability to connect explicit instruction and its resultant knowledge with acquisition as defined more broadly by scholars in the field. Some scholars argue, however, that there is a benefit to explicit knowledge because it can influence the development of implicit knowledge in some way. The claim is that there is an interface between explicit and implicit knowledge. This is speculation, at best, and there is no empirical evidence that this is so. One problem with this position is that there is no qualitative difference between explicit and implicit knowledge made by such scholars—they are essentially the same thing (e.g., an explicit textbook rule is what winds up in a learner's head implicitly). But we have repeatedly said that what exists in our heads as language, whether a first or second language, is an implicit mental representation distinct from explicit knowledge. Our position, then, is that there cannot be an interface between explicit knowledge and implicit mental representation. There are many problems in positing an interface that have not been addressed. The major one is that the concept of interface is not defined. Just what is an interface, and how does it work? What linguistic or psychological mechanisms are involved? We will revisit the interface idea when we elaborate on why explicit knowledge can't turn into implicit mental representation.

These caveats are problems for almost all of the research on the effects of instruction on acquisition, regardless of the type of instruction, where it is conducted, who the learners are, and so on. The caveats are so important that they essentially undermine any conclusions a person would like to make that explicit teaching and learning are somehow either useful or necessary for acquisition. As the research moves forward, the nature of language and the measurements of learning will need to be more carefully considered. With increasing access to neurolinguistic tools such as electroencephalography and magnetoencephalography, researchers may be able to make significant advancements in terms of distinguishing explicit and implicit learning and resultant explicit knowledge and implicit mental representation. Again, the use of such tools is dependent on how researchers define language and mental representation.

Long-Term Effects of Instruction

A major issue in research about whether instruction impacts acquisition has to do with short- versus long-term effects. Short-term effects refer to the comparison of pretest and posttest scores immediately or very soon after instruction. Long-term effects refer to the comparison of test scores after some time has elapsed. How much time? That's a good question. Bill VanPatten and Claudia Fernández showed in a 2004 publication that up until that time, only five studies had looked at the effects of instruction as long as a year later. They showed that the effects of instruction had disappeared in all of the cases.

Quick Reflection

Teachers often comment that their students have "forgotten everything from the year before." Has this been your experience? How might you reconcile that observation with what you are reading here?

A more recent study is revealing. In 2019, Mari Umeda and her colleagues set out to investigate the L2 acquisition of English articles by native Japanese speakers. Japanese does not have definite or indefinite articles, so when Japanese speakers encounter them in L2 English, they cannot rely on L1 knowledge to help them understand their function. The use of English articles is actually quite complex. Determining whether to use a definite article (*the*), indefinite article (*a*, *an*), or no article depends on the interplay of various abstract features. Here is an example of how Umeda and her colleagues tested learners' knowledge of how articles work:

Prompt 1: I know that you like birds. Well, if you ever visit California, you'll see different kinds of birds there. For example, I found out ...

a. the pelican lives on the California coast.
b. pelicans live on the California coast.
c. a pelican lives on the California coast.
d. the pelicans live on the California coast.
e. pelican lives on the California coast.

You have likely concluded that choices (a) and (b) are the most natural and that the other three options sound quite bad. In this study, a group of L2 English learners took a pretest. They performed poorly, suggesting little to no knowledge about articles. Then they received explicit instruction on the use of English articles over the course of 9 weeks and completed four posttests at different points after instruction ended: at Week 3, at Week 10, at Week 22, and finally at 1 year and 22 weeks. The results showed that scores at Weeks 3 and 10 were higher than scores on the pretests. However, at Week 22, learners' scores dropped significantly, and there was only a lingering effect of explicit instruction. Finally, at 1 year and 22 weeks later, there was no longer any measurable effect. The scores had regressed to the point of being statistically indistinguishable from the pretest scores.

A reasonable conclusion from this study is that explicit instruction results in short-term effects for explicit knowledge, not for implicit mental representation. We have no real evidence to conclude that explicit instruction provides L2 learners with something that affects their acquisition in the long run. We are back to the idea that we have argued previously. Learners—or, better yet, their internal mechanisms—are in charge of acquisition. And central to that acquisition are implicit processes out of the reach of instructors and materials.

Explicit instruction results in short-term effects for explicit knowledge, not for implicit mental representation.

Potential Negative Effects of Explicit Teaching and Explicit Learning

In some cases, explicit teaching and learning are shown to have negative consequences. We will look at two classic examples.

Manfred Pienemann has developed a theory of L2 output processing that describes and predicts ordered development. His original research focused on the acquisition of German word order, which differs from languages like English, Spanish, and Mandarin Chinese because of what is called "verb second" position. In a nutshell, inflected verbs (verbs with endings that indicate tense) always appear in the second position of a simple sentence, while in embedded clauses they appear at the end. With compound verbs such as "have gone," *have* would appear in second position in a simple sentence, while *gone* would appear later, typically at the end. In embedded clauses, *have* would appear at the end of the clause. Here are sentences to illustrate. (To make the changes in German word order more apparent, the second line in each example shows the literal word-for-word translation in English. The third line represents the standard translation in English. Although we use *have* in the English translation of these sentences, German uses the verb *be* with verbs such as *go*.)

(7) Ich gehe zur Uni.
I go to school.
'I go to school.'

(8) Dann gehe ich zur Uni.
Then go I to school.
'Then I go to school.'

(9) Ich bin zur Uni gegangen.
I am to school gone.
'I have gone to school.'

(10) Er denkt, dass ich zur Uni gehe.
He thinks that I to school go.
'He thinks that I go to school.'

(11) Er denkt, dass ich zur Uni gegangen bin.
He thinks that I to school gone am.
'He thinks that I have gone to school.'

Research on the acquisition of German has revealed that there is staged development in the acquisition of German word order. In one experiment, Pienemann tried to teach learners of German to skip stages (e.g., they were at Stage 2 and he tried to make them acquire Stage 4). What he found was that none of the learners could do this, and some of them regressed to a previous stage, suggesting negative effects of the instruction. This led Pienemann to develop what he called the Teachability Hypothesis, which basically says we can't make learners do something they're not ready to do naturally. Let's turn our attention to another example of the potential negative effects of explicitly learning rules.

The Teachability Hypothesis basically says we can't make learners do something they're not ready to do naturally.

L2 learners of Spanish usually take many years to acquire the expression of past tense. Spanish encodes grammatical aspect on verbs in the past tense. Grammatical aspect is a linguistic device indicating how an action or state is viewed relative to a point in time. Generally speaking, *perfective aspect* is used to highlight that an event has a clear-cut beginning and/or end (e.g., "I ate a sandwich"). By contrast, *imperfective aspect* is used when there is no reference to the beginning or end of an event ("I was eating a sandwich"; "I used to eat sandwiches a lot as a kid"). In Spanish, these two perspectives result in different verb endings: *Comí un sándwich* 'I ate a sandwich' vs. *comía un sandwich* 'I was eating a sandwich.' The first is called the preterit and the second is called the imperfect. In addition to grammatical aspect, every verb also has its own lexical aspect. For example, the state of "being a human" is temporally very different from a shorter but durative action such as *run*, which in turn is different from a quick action like *blink*. And verbs can combine with other phrases that change their durative nature, as in *run* versus "run a mile." The addition of *a mile* adds an end point to the more general concept of running.

The complex interplay of these various factors makes it difficult for L2 learners to acquire aspectual differences in a nativelike way without years of input and interaction with that input.

Textbooks attempt to reduce the complexity of expressing the past into simple rules. What happens when learners diligently work at learning such rules? Jason Rothman researched the development of past tense expression in two groups of advanced L2 Spanish learners. One group learned Spanish primarily in the classroom with explicit instruction, and another group learned Spanish implicitly through natural exposure in Spain, without ever studying Spanish formally. A group of native Spanish speakers also participated in the study to serve as a benchmark for target language use. All three groups were given a Spanish version of *Goldilocks and the Three Bears*, and they had to decide whether the preterit or imperfect form of verbs was most appropriate based on context.

After analyzing the preterit and imperfect choices of all groups, Rothman found that the group of L2 learners who learned Spanish implicitly by living in Spain performed like the native speaker group. There was no significant difference between their selection of verb forms. The group of L2 classroom learners who were accustomed to explicit instruction performed worse than both the native speakers and L2 non-classroom learners. The classroom learners chose inappropriate verb forms with higher frequency, and these inappropriate choices could be directly linked to the simplistic grammar rules they had learned from textbooks and teachers.

Two important conclusions can be drawn from Rothman's study. First, L2 learners can develop nativelike knowledge of even highly complex phenomena, such as aspectual contrast, without receiving instruction. Second, it is possible for people who learn an L2 without instruction to develop knowledge that is more nativelike than the knowledge of people who learn an L2 with instruction. The latter conclusion is particularly important as additional evidence for the centrality of implicit learning in L2 acquisition.

In a Nutshell ...

Research on explicit and implicit teaching is fraught with problems and should not lead us to conclude that explicit teaching and learning are either beneficial or necessary. In addition, research on explicit teaching and learning strongly suggests that the effects are (a) short term and (b) biased for explicit knowledge, not implicit mental representation. Finally, there is some evidence that explicit teaching and learning can have negative effects on development.

Based on what you've read so far, what would you say about the applicability of the following common adage to language acquisition? "Practice makes perfect."

Two Final Comments

Explicit Knowledge Cannot Turn into Implicit Representation

In 1993, Bonnie Schwartz wrote an important theoretical essay in which she argued that explicit information—including explicit rules and error correction—is ineffectual for building an underlying mental representation of language. In other words, explicit knowledge cannot build or turn into implicit knowledge. To make her point, she argued that if the development of an implicit language system were based on explicit knowledge, L2 learners could acquire language using simple hypothesis-testing procedures and error correction. For example, teachers could tell their learners how the L2 works, and learners would follow that pattern. If that pattern were to fail and the learners made an error, the teacher would point out the error to the student, and the student would cease to make that error. Language acquisition would be efficient and directly reflect the sequence in which concepts were taught. But this is not how language acquisition works, as we saw in Chapter 2. In a 2016 essay, Bill VanPatten echoed these ideas examining recent research on German. We'll take his ideas here and revisit one phenomenon involving word order in German.

Let's look at a simple sentence in German. Here are sentences repeated from an earlier section:

(12) Ich gehe zur Uni.
'I go to school.'

(13) Dann gehe ich zur Uni.
'Then I go to school.'

Although teachers and others characterize German as a subject-verb-object language, linguists consider it a subject-object-verb language. What happens is that both the subject and the verb move from their positions inside the VP and higher up to get word order in a non-embedded sentence. (For our purposes, we are ignoring the theoretical motivation for why certain elements move.) If we drew a tree the way linguists do to depict what underlies sentence (12), it would look like Figure 4.1. (*Note:* We have removed one of the phrases [DP] for simplification in the figure.)

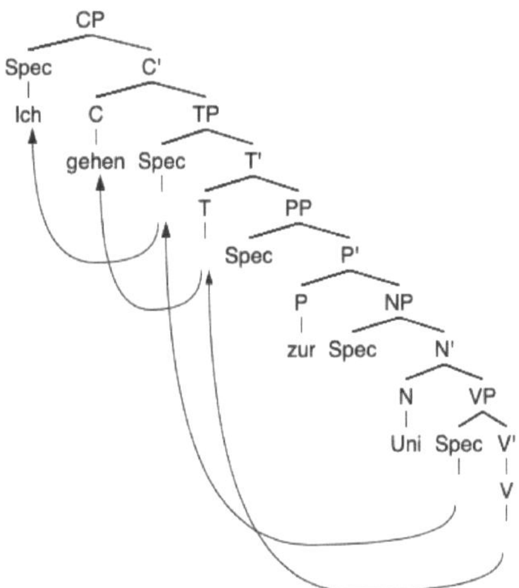

Figure 4.1. Depiction of Movement of Elements in a Simple German Sentence

Figure 4.2 illustrates what happens when an adverb is added in the sentence.

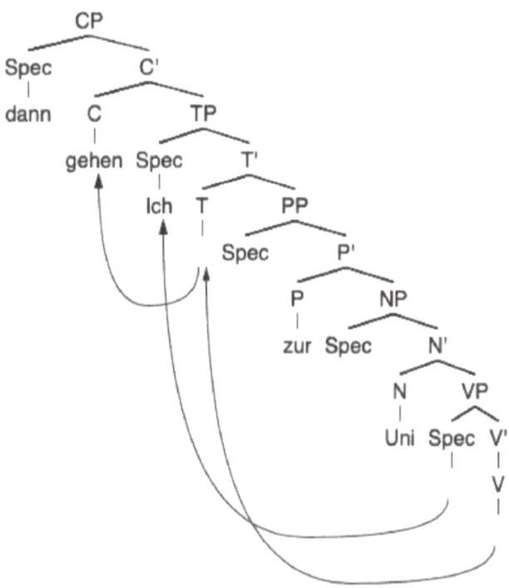

Figure 4.2. Depiction of Movement of Elements in a Simple Sentence in German with an Adverb

When *dann* is inserted into its spot, it blocks movement of the subject. That is, like the rule in physics says, no two objects can occupy the same spot at the same time. *Ich* cannot move up to the highest part of the sentence. However, nothing blocks the movement of the verb, and this is how German gets its characteristic "verb in second position" structure in main sentences.

Hopefully your eyes haven't crossed from looking at all of the movement of elements in a sentence! But what we see here is that what learners are taught, as "the verb must be in second position" is a result of movement of elements.

This may all seem esoteric to you. And if you ask, "How do we even know this happens?" you would be right to ask that question. Unfortunately, this is not the place to entertain the motivation in theoretical linguistics for why movement happens. The takeaway is this: Textbook rules are one thing, and mental representation is another. They are qualitatively different. Like the adage "You can't make a silk purse out of a sow's ear," explicit information cannot turn into

Textbooks rules are one thing, and mental representation is another. They are qualitatively different.

implicit mental representation. There is no mechanism for this transformation in language. Mental representation is always the result of the interaction between communicatively embedded input and the learner's internal mechanisms that process and organize language.

It may help to think of the difference between explicit and implicit knowledge with a car metaphor. Non-electric cars run on gasoline only. If someone puts vinegar in the gas tank, the car will store it, and the gas gauge will even show that the tank is full, but the car will not run. Language is developed implicitly in our brain based on abstract data from communicatively embedded input. This is the only fuel our brain can process to build language. We can fill learners' brains with lots of explicit rules, but this explicit knowledge is like vinegar in a gas tank.

Quick Reflection

Has the discussion so far given you pause to think about the rules in textbooks? If so, how? If not, why not?

Before leaving this section, we would like to touch briefly on an alternative to linguistic theory: usage-based approaches. In these approaches, mental representation for language is also the result of implicit processes, even though they do not characterize language as we do in this book. But like the position taken here, these approaches, too, would argue that explicit information cannot turn into implicit mental representation. Why? Because in usage-based approaches, what resides in our heads is a complex network of connections and constructions. This network is the result of the way the mind tallies the frequency of occurrences in communicatively embedded input and, subsequently, how this information is organized and stored. This network is also qualitatively different from explicit knowledge, and, as in the case of linguistic theory, there is no known mechanism that can turn explicit knowledge into implicit mental representation.

A Limited Role for Explicit Learning

We hope it's now clear that explicit learning does not play a major role in language acquisition; in fact, it cannot. Based on the abstract and complex nature of language, there does not appear to be a mechanism that would allow deficient explicit knowledge to aid in the development of an implicit language system. However, is this true for all aspects of language? Some scholars have suggested that perhaps vocabulary can be acquired explicitly, even if the formal properties of language cannot. We touched on this in an earlier part of this chapter when we looked at what learners must encode on words when learning them. To remind ourselves, the word *viven* in Spanish means "they live." But there's much more to this word than its meaning. We repeat what we listed before:

- [meaning: something about living]
- [the sounds]
- [-N], [+V]: The word is a verb and not a noun or something else.
- [3rd]: The reference is to third person.
- [+plural]: The reference is to more than one entity.
- [+ present, -past]: The time frame is present.

The point is that even vocabulary words have formal features, and many decades of psychological and linguistic research have shown that our knowledge of words is complex and implicit. For example, when we are shown an image of a word—perhaps *computer*—we also mentally activate other related words, such as *keyboard*, *mouse*, *screen*, and *internet*. This activation happens automatically, without awareness. The frequency of words is also tallied mentally in an implicit way. Considering something else, have you ever experienced what is called a "tip of the tongue" phenomenon? When a word is on the "tip of someone's tongue," that person generally can't retrieve the whole word, but research has shown the person can still retrieve features of the word, such as the first letter, the syllabic stress, the meaning, or words that sound similarly. This demonstrates that we break down words into many different components, which is something that we certainly don't do consciously.

Although not central to the acquisition of formal properties of language, learners may still engage in some explicit learning during comprehension when it comes to trying to figure out the basic meaning of something. For example, when they hear a word they don't know, they generally try to attribute meaning to it, and this may occur explicitly. Let's say learners hear the unknown French word *ordinateur*. They might consciously think, "I don't know this word," yet, at the same time, they may consciously make use of the context in which the word appears and say to themselves, "Oh! That means *computer*." In this instance, the meaning is somehow arrived at explicitly. However, this explicit focus on meaning happens independently of the implicit processes in which the learner engages, which include considering how frequent the word is, a mental activation of all the other French words related to it, the fact that it's a noun, the fact that it's a count noun, its singular form, the sequences of sounds, and so on.

Learners may still engage in some explicit learning when it comes to trying to figure out the basic meaning of something.

Our point, then, is this: Implicit processes are central to how the formal properties of language are acquired and develop over time; explicit learning and processing are most likely relegated to how learners grapple with the surface meaning of words and phrases. This is why learners sometimes get lost in a longer utterance they hear. If they are trying to figure out the meaning of a word or phrase early in the utterance, the rest of the utterance keeps coming and they miss it. Explicit processing during comprehension takes up a lot of working memory. Once we get stuck on a word, we jam up the comprehension capacity for the rest of the sentence.

In a Nutshell ...

Because there are no known or posited mechanisms to do this, explicit knowledge cannot turn into implicit mental representation of language. Explicit learning may be implicated in how learners try to figure out what a word or phrase means but not what the formal properties of language are.

Consider asking your students the following question or making it a brief essay assignment: "How are languages learned?" What do they say? Why do you think they respond as they do? Alternatively, do you engage them in discussion about what it means to acquire a language? What are those discussions like?

Summary

Scholars of language acquisition agree that the ultimate goal in language acquisition is to develop an implicit language system. Although it has become popular in research to compare explicit and implicit learning as two equally plausible pathways for language acquisition, there is an extensive amount of theoretical and empirical research that indicates that explicit learning cannot have a major role in the development of an implicit language system. Most research that has indicated that explicit learning has a positive effect on learning has likely not accounted for the caveats that we described in this chapter. Or, in some cases, the conclusions of this research rest on theoretical assumptions that do not fully consider the complex and abstract nature of language. If we zoom out and look at decades of research on ordered development, we can see that explicit learning and instruction are not able to affect the fundamental processes and patterns in language acquisition. As it currently stands, the standard assumption should be that implicit learning is central in acquisition and explicit learning plays a limited role. Understanding and defining this limited role is a worthy focus of future research, but it should be clear that implicit learning remains central.

Selected References and Suggested Readings

For an expanded and detailed treatment of the issues raised in this chapter, please consult the following book, which is part of the publisher's Elements series:

VanPatten, B., & Smith, M. (2022). *Explicit and implicit learning in second language acquisition*. Cambridge University Press.

For a summary of research in psychology on explicit and implicit learning, we suggest the following books:

Cleeremans, A., Allakhverdov, V., & Kuvaldina, M. (Eds.). (2019). Implicit learning: 50 years on. Routledge.

Reber, A. S. (1993). Implicit learning and tacit knowledge: An essay on the cognitive unconscious. Oxford University Press.

We also recommend these resources for an overview of implicit learning in L2 acquisition:

Rebuschat, P. (Ed.). (2015). *Implicit and explicit learning of languages.* John Benjamins.

Williams, J. (2009). Implicit learning in second language acquisition. In W. Ritchie & T. K. Bhatia (Eds.), *The new handbook of second language acquisition* (pp. 319–355). Emerald Group Publishing.

You might also wish to peruse this volume to see how different approaches to L2 acquisition treat the explicit/implicit issue:

VanPatten, B., Keating, G. D., & Wulff, S. (Eds.). (2020). *Theories in second language acquisition* (3rd ed.). Routledge.

Here is a non-exhaustive list of resources that cover classic research on how ordered development is not affected by explicit learning and instruction. We've selected these readings because they've stood the test of time.

Ellis, R. (1989). Are classroom and naturalistic acquisition the same? *Studies in Second Language Acquisition*, *11*, 305–328.

Lightbown, P. M. (1983). Exploring relationships between developmental and instructional sequences in L2 acquisition. In H. Seliger & M. Long (Eds.), *Classroom-oriented research in second language acquisition* (pp. 217–243). Newbury House.

Pavesi, M. (1986). Markedness, discoursal modes and relative clause formation in a formal and informal context. *Studies in Second Language Acquisition*, *8*, 38–53.

Pica, T. (1983). Adult acquisition of English as a second language under different conditions of exposure. *Language Learning*, *33*, 465–497.

Schumann, J. (1978). *The pidginization process.* Newbury House.

In this chapter, we referred to a number of meta-analyses on the effects of instruction and explicit learning:

Goo, J., Granena, G., Yilmaz, Y., & Novella, M. (2015). Implicit and explicit instruction in L2 learning: Norris and Ortega (2000) revisited and updated. In P. Rebuschat (Ed.), *Implicit and explicit learning of languages* (pp. 443–482). John Benjamins.

Kang, E. Y., Sok, S., & Han, Z. (2019). Thirty-five years of ISLA on form-focused instruction: A meta-analysis. *Language Teaching Research, 23*(4), 428–453.

Norris, J., & Ortega, L. (2000). Effectiveness of second language instruction: A research synthesis and quantitative meta-analysis. *Language Learning, 50*, 417–528.

Spada, N., & Tomita, Y. (2010). Interactions between type of instruction and type of language feature: A meta-analysis. *Language Learning, 60*(2), 263–308.

If you'd like to examine some research on how explicit information cannot turn into implicit mental representation, we suggest the following readings:

Schwartz, B. (1993). On explicit and negative data effecting and affecting competence and linguistic behavior. *Studies in Second Language Acquisition, 15*(2), 147–163.

VanPatten, B. (2016). Why explicit information cannot become implicit knowledge. *Foreign Language Annals, 49*(4), 650–657.

Wu, M.-J., & Ionin, T. (2022). Does explicit instruction affect L2 linguistic competence? An examination with L2 acquisition of English inverse scope. *Second Language Research, 38*(3), 607–637. https://doi.org/10.1177%2F0267658321992830

Finally, here are additional readings and research we mentioned in the chapter:

Pienemann, M. (1984). Psychological constraints on the teachability of languages. *Studies in Second Language Acquisition, 6*, 186–214.

Rothman, J. (2008). Aspect selection in adult L2 Spanish and the Competing Systems Hypothesis. *Languages in Contrast, 8*(1), 74–106.

Umeda, M., Snape, N., & Yusa, N. (2019). The long-term effect of explicit instruction on learners' knowledge of English articles. *Language Teaching Research, 23*, 179–199.

VanPatten, B., & Fernández, C. (2004). The long-term effects of processing instruction. In B. VanPatten (Ed.), *Processing instruction: Theory, research, and commentary* (pp. 273–289). Erlbaum.

Thinking Some More

1. Return to the "Before You Read" box at the beginning of the chapter. What do you think of the statements now? Has anything in your mind changed?
2. List three to five takeaways from this chapter. Which of these might be most useful for a novice teacher to know? Which takeaways do you think would make for good discussion with colleagues where you teach or will teach?
3. When we say that ordered development is not affected by explicit instruction or explicit learning, we mean that stages and the order in which things are acquired do not change. However, some research suggests that instruction might have an impact on what learners do at a given stage or with a given structure. As an example, read the articles by Pica and Pavesi listed in Selected References and Suggested Readings and determine to what extent you think the results support the statement that explicit instruction and explicit learning are necessary or central to acquisition.
4. It surprises some teachers to hear that explicit instruction and learning can have negative effects on acquisition. Review the section of this chapter called "Potential Negative Effects of Explicit Teaching and Explicit Learning," then decide which of the following statements makes the most sense to you in understanding such negative effects as you consider all that you've read in this book:
    - Learners misapply rules.
    - Learners don't learn the rules well.
    - The rules are inadequate and lead learners astray.
    - The rules cause learners to process input incorrectly.
5. Review the idea of Poverty of the Stimulus (POS) situation. Try coming up with a 100-word summary of POS to share with others.

6. A recurring theme in this book is that we all need to grapple with the nature of language and that textbook rules and charts do not represent what winds up in our heads. See if you can list three or four reasons why understanding the nature of language can be useful for both discussion among colleagues and curricular innovation. If you don't believe it can be useful, explain why not.

Considering the Classroom

1. Give learners a standard test on something grammatical they have explicitly learned. Then, on another day, ask them to do a timed writing (e.g., "You have 10 minutes to write 100 words."). Compare their performance. What conclusion can you draw regarding their learning?
2. If you are convinced that implicit learning is central to language acquisition, which of the following statements makes the most sense for your classroom now?
    - Eliminate explicit teaching and learning altogether.
    - Minimize explicit teaching and learning in some way.
    - Only make explicit references to language when learners ask you a question about something.
    - Eliminate explicit teaching and learning in the early and intermediate stages and bring some in at the more advanced stages (or the reverse).
    - Eliminate explicit teaching and learning regarding oral language development, but provide some when it comes to developing writing abilities.

    If you come up with some other ideas, excellent!
3. Imagine you are not focused on explicit teaching and learning all that much. You notice that your second-year learners cannot produce something "simple" with any accuracy. Do you worry about it and try to push things along with some explicit teaching and learning? Do you let it go, knowing it will eventually take care of itself? Do you have some other strategy? To what extent does your knowledge of how language is acquired affect your decision-making?

4. Consider making a list of 10 things every student should know about L2 acquisition to post in your classroom and use for occasional discussion. Now that you have finished the first four chapters of this book, what would you include on that list?

FAQs

If you'd like, go to Chapter 5, "Frequently Asked Questions," and check out the following questions that are related to topics in this chapter. (The numbers match the numbers for the questions in Chapter 5.)

11. Don't imitation and repetition play a role in acquisition?
12. Doesn't giving learners rules help? (That's the way I learned ...)
13. What about social factors? Don't they affect acquisition in a significant way?
14. Don't different levels of learners need different things to help them keep learning?

5

Chapter 5

Frequently Asked Questions

Teachers constantly have to make decisions.
The best teachers are those who make informed decisions.

Before You Read

Make a list of any lingering questions you have after reading Chapters 1 through 4.

We have both engaged in a number of efforts over the years to interact with teachers about language, language acquisition, and related matters. These efforts include workshops, presentations, courses, and the live podcasts and call-in radio shows *Tea with BVP* and *Talkin' L2 with BVP*. Such interactions always include questions from teachers and teachers-in-training. In this chapter, we have gathered 15 of the most frequently asked questions related to language acquisition. We don't intend for this chapter to be exhaustive, but we do hope to address some of the questions you may have after reading the previous chapters. This chapter is longer than the others, but that's on purpose. In a sense, each question is like a mini chapter that stands alone. You may skip around any way you'd like unless you decide to simply go through them one by one. Alternatively, you may have already looked at particular questions as they were referenced at the end of Chapters 1 through 4.

Let's begin!

1. Are some languages more difficult to learn than others?

Because the two of us are associated with teaching Spanish, we sometimes hear from administrators, parents, colleagues (including language teachers), and even students that we teach "an easy language." We don't teach one of the "hard" languages like Russian, Chinese, or Arabic. The idea that languages fall on a continuum of easy to hard is a staple in folklore—and it is perpetuated by unpublished data from sources such as the Foreign Service Institute, which has classified languages into four groups from easiest to most difficult based on the time it takes to reach a certain level of proficiency. Is there something to this idea that some languages are more difficult than others? The answer depends on what you're looking at. But before we look at L2 acquisition, let's think about child language acquisition for a moment.

One of us once posed the question to a colleague who was a well-known researcher in child L1 acquisition. She scoffed at the idea that some languages are easier or more difficult. In a nutshell, she said that languages balance out so that each language has some things that are easy for that language and some things that are hard for that language. If languages were not on a level playing field, children couldn't acquire them. Indeed, if one scours the literature on child L1 acquisition, there is no discussion about language X being more difficult than language Y. It's just not a notion that preoccupies L1 researchers (although they are interested in why some aspects of a particular language are acquired later than others, but that's a different FAQ in this chapter).

Turning our attention to L2 acquisition, we would argue that the same is true: No language is more difficult than another and each language presents its own easy and hard "stuff." We are, of course, referring to the development of language in the head, or what we have repeatedly referred to as mental representation. So, when a Russian teacher says, "Oh, yes, but Russian is hard because of our crazy case system," one response could be "Yes, Chinese lacks case but has a tone system. L2 learners struggle with that along with their crazy classifier system for nouns. Yes, Spanish doesn't have a case system, but it has differential object marking. Differential object marking takes a long time to acquire. And Spanish also has a crazy verbal inflection system that takes lots of time to get under control. Yes, English doesn't mark case on nouns, but it has a crazy auxiliary and modal system along with some other syntactic rules that defy easy description." What we teasingly underscore in this response is the same thing that is underscored in L1 acquisition: Languages operate on a level playing field, or they wouldn't be acquirable. Each language has easier and more difficult aspects to acquire, but no language is, in essence, more difficult than another.

Quick Reflection

What aspects of the language you teach seem difficult for your learners? Why do you think they are difficult?

Teachers and some scholars in the profession might still argue that some languages are harder than others for, say, English speakers. The question we ask is, "Where does this perception come from?" We think it comes from a number of sources. One source, for some languages, is that if there are no readily discernible cognates, then it's tougher to begin to map meaning onto form. So, Spanish seems easier because it has a number of readily identifiable cognates with English (e.g., *transportation* = *transportación*; *family* = *familia*), but Chinese does not (*transportation* = *yùnshū*; *family* = *jiātíng*). Teachers of Mandarin thus can't use cognates to facilitate communication in the classroom—and communication is essential to acquisition, as we saw in Chapter 3 and elsewhere. We are not considering here the problem of false cognates—words that look alike but mean different things. Take the Spanish word *actual*, which may cause initial confusion for English speakers because it means "current," as in "current news."

Another source of the idea that some languages are more difficult than others for English speakers may be the literacy and writing system. Because L2 learners of world languages in the United States are typically literate in English, teachers can rely on their knowledge of spelling and word recognition when teaching Spanish, French, and even German, for example. This is not possible with Arabic, Japanese, or Korean. Reports that it takes longer to learn Chinese than Spanish are in part due to the fact that it takes longer to become literate in Chinese than it does Spanish (e.g., teachers and students spend as much time mastering characters as they do engaging in language acquisition). But literacy and acquisition of language are two different things, because it is certainly possible to acquire a language without developing literacy in it. And, of course, humans as a species had language long before they had literacy. Yet teachers and organizations like the Foreign Service Institute (FSI) conflate these ideas when they look at how long it takes to learn a language. If you took written language out of the equation and conducted an experiment with Spanish and Chinese, in which you focused on only aural input and interaction, you might find that the time differences referenced in the FSI charts are reduced considerably or maybe even disappear. What you might see, for example, is that early on, learners of Spanish might accelerate compared with learners of Chinese in part due to the issue of cognates, as mentioned previously. But as time moved on, you would see that the mental representation of learners of Chinese catches up with that of learners of Spanish regarding how sounds and words work in their new language.

Quick Reflection

Would you ever consider teaching a beginning language course and not using written materials at all until learners are much further along? How difficult or easy might that be?

An additional source of the perception of relative difficulty comes from teachers themselves. If they have been convinced or trained to believe their language is difficult, they may make the learning of it more difficult than it needs to be. Let's return to Russian for a moment. Because many Russian teachers believe the case system is hard to acquire, they feel the need to explicitly teach it and have learners practice it. They do so at the expense of input and interaction in the classroom. This approach slows down acquisition in the long run, thus causing learners to take more time as their access to input and interaction is reduced or minimized. And, of course, the Russian teachers often neglect the fact that little kids learning Russian as an L1 get the case system pretty well without teaching, albeit showing patterns of ordered development such as those we discussed in Chapter 2.

With this said, it's critical to point out that the issue of difficulty is framed completely from the English speaker's point of view. That is, Chinese is "harder" for the English speaker than Spanish. But what happens if you are dealing with the Japanese speaker? Maybe suddenly Spanish is more difficult than, say, Korean. Or maybe for the Japanese speaker, English and Spanish are equally difficult. When we begin to look beyond the English speaker's point of view, we see exactly what the L1 acquisitionists say: Languages exist on a level playing field when it comes to acquisition, and some things in one language are easy to learn, while others are difficult. In another language, it may be a different set of things that are either easy or difficult. But like L1 acquisitionists, L2 acquisitionists who look at how language itself is acquired don't focus on literacy or even communicative ability, as these lie outside the strict domain of language. This is important to keep in mind. So, it could be that Japanese is more difficult than Spanish for English speakers when it comes to bootstrapping yourself into some kind of communicative ability but not because the formal system of language is more difficult. Instead, Japanese may be more difficult because how people communicate in Japanese may have less overlap with how English speakers communicate compared with how Spanish speakers communicate. We are speculating here, to be sure, but our point should not be missed: Language, literacy, and communication are three distinct things. We shouldn't confuse and conflate them when we talk about one *language* being more difficult than another.

One final note: We are focused on the acquisition of language here, meaning the formal properties that we outlined in Chapter 1. In terms of communication, there could be real differences in how long it takes to become communicatively competent in a language (leaving aside, for the moment, what *communicatively competent* actually means). Cultural differences and norms of communicative behavior may elude learners for a variety of reasons. For example, a colleague of ours who is a native speaker of English lived in Japan for several years. Although she is fluent in Japanese, she reported that it took her a long time to find people to interact with because she sensed Japanese society tended to be closed to outsiders. This could have been her perception, or it could have been something real. The point is that her lack of interaction with others impeded the development of her communicative ability, along with the social and cultural practices that may be reflected in communication. This, in turn, may include cultural nuances of meaning for words and phrases that can only be learned in context. A *sensei* in Japanese may translate as *teacher* in English, but do American and Japanese cultures imbue their respective words with the exact same social and political attributes?

Unfortunately, there are no references we can offer on this topic. However, the following resource is a good speculative essay on the subject:

Polio, C. (2016). Are some languages really more difficult to learn? Maybe, maybe not. *CLEAR*, *20*(2), 1–5. (*Note:* CLEAR is the acronym for the Center for Language Education and Research at Michigan State University.)

2. What makes some structures difficult to acquire and others easy?

We often hear teachers lament that the subjunctive in Spanish is difficult compared with the indicative, or that the case system in Russian is difficult compared with present tense verb endings, or the tone system in Chinese is difficult compared with sentence structure. What they report is how learners struggle to "master" such things. Teachers often attribute the difficulty to L1 differences: There is no subjunctive in English, there is no complex case system in English, and there is no tone system in English. Although there may be some aspects of L1 influence on L2 acquisition (see the FAQ on the role of the L1), difficulty is often inherent in a language and not necessarily due to L1/L2 differences. Why would we say this?

First, in child L1 acquisition, there are easy and difficult things—or, put differently, there are things that are acquired earlier or later than others. Yet children don't have an L1 that is "getting in the way." In the English sound system, bilabials (/m/ /b/ /p/) are acquired quite early by children, as are basic vowels, whereas rhotics (/r/) are acquired much later. So, for example, early on, *momma* and *papa* are easy and sound adultlike, but *rabbit* comes out as "wabit." Passive sentences ("The boy was chased by the doggie") aren't fully acquired until a child is well into elementary school. And research shows that some aspects of language aren't adultlike for L1 learners until puberty! Research on Spanish, Russian, and Chinese children reveal the same thing: Some things are acquired early (easy), and some things are acquired much later (more difficult). So, there is something about properties of languages themselves that comes into play with regard to what makes something easier or more difficult.

The same is true for L2 acquisition. Some inherent properties of language make some aspects of them easier or more difficult to acquire—and this plays out in terms of the time course of acquisition (earlier acquired versus later acquired). What are some of those properties?

- *Inherent complexity 1.* Some things in language have multiple functions and/or meanings. The simplest and easiest things are those in which one form or one structure is equal to one and only one meaning. In Japanese, *o* marks objects and only objects of verbs. This makes it a relatively easy particle in Japanese. In Spanish, *a* can be a preposition of direction ("to" a place), a preposition of destination or goal ("to" or "for" someone), and a direct object marker (*El coyote persigue a la oveja* 'The coyote is chasing the sheep'). This multifunctional use of one little word complicates the acquisition of some of its functions.

- *Inherent complexity 2*. Some things in language combine several features so that one form or structure has more than one grammatical property. An example of this would be the Russian case system. Case endings on nouns in Russian combine three distinct features: case (there are six of them, including nominative, accusative, and instrumental), declension (there are three classes of nouns with different endings; gender is a feature in one declension), and number (singular versus plural, also with different endings). Another example would be the so-called "personal *a*" in Spanish. That it is called personal *a* in textbooks and online programs belies the complexity underlying its use. We don't simply use the personal *a* to mark people as objects of the verb (e.g., *Russ conoce a Bill* 'Russ knows Bill). Whether or not an object is marked with *a* depends on a complex interplay of animacy, definiteness, specificity, pragmatic factors, and others (linguists still haven't concluded what all the factors are). See the example in the discussion of inherent complexity 1 involving the coyote and the sheep. Coyotes and sheep aren't people.
- *Transparency in meaning*. Things with easily transparent meaning attached to them are easier than things with less transparent meaning or no meaning. In English, lexical verbs such as *eat*, *hit*, *run*, and *see* are easier to acquire than the auxiliary verb *do*, which has no inherent meaning and serves a purely grammatical function (e.g., to carry tense, to carry person-number features).
- *Frequency*. Things that are used more frequently tend to be acquired sooner than things that are used less frequently. In languages like Spanish and French, masculine nouns are much more frequently used than feminine nouns, meaning that adjective agreement with nouns tends to follow a path in which agreement with masculine nouns precedes the acquisition of agreement with feminine nouns. In other words, feminine agreement is more difficult than masculine agreement.

- *Operations across boundaries*. Things that don't require grammatical operations across boundaries are easier to acquire than things that do. In languages that have such things as agreement (e.g., subject-verb, noun-adjective), agreement is easier when it doesn't cross a phrase boundary or only crosses one phrase boundary, but it is much more difficult than agreement that crosses a clause boundary. Here is an example from French:

  $[_{TP}$ J'habite $[_{PP}$ dans $[_{DP}$ une $[_{NP}$ **maison blanche**]]]] 'I live in a white house': Agreement is "easy" between *maison* and *blanche* because they are in the same syntactic phrase.

  $[_{TP}$ Je connais $[_{DP}$ la $[_{NP}$ **maison** $[_{CP}$ que $[_{TP}$ t'as $[_{ADJ}$ **décrite**]]]]]] 'I know the house that you've described': Agreement between *maison* and *décrite* is harder in this example because the agreement has to cross multiple phrase boundaries, including a clause boundary indicated by $[_{CP}]$.

- *Interfaces*. Because language consists of different formal components, there may be interfaces between them. Syntax (constraints on elements in a sentence) is one component, and discourse (constraints on how sentences work together to make meaning) is another. But there can be an interface between these components. A classic example comes from Italian and Spanish. Both Italian and Spanish allow null subjects and overt subject pronouns so that *parla* or *habla* 'talks' is possible and *lui parla* or *él habla* 'he talks' is possible. That Spanish and Italian allow null subjects is easy for learners to acquire. It is a purely syntactic phenomenon. However, there is an interface between syntax and discourse such that the distribution of null and overt subjects is not the same. Both languages, for example, have a strong tendency for a null subject of a second clause or sentence to take the subject of the previous clause or sentence as the subject, even though syntactically there is no constraint on this. Thus, *Giovanni ha visto Luigi dopo che é ritornato/lui é ritornato d'Italia* and *Juan vio a Luís después que regresó/él regresó de Italia* 'John saw Louis after he returned from Italy' are both possible syntactically. Yet speakers of Italian and Spanish would say that John returned from Italy in the case of *é ritornato/regresó* (null subject) and would prefer to link Louis to returning from Italy when there is an overt subject pronoun in the second clause, *lui é ritornato/él regresó*. This distribution of subject pronoun antecedent preference in Italian and Spanish (and similar languages) seems to take both L1 learners and L2 learners a long time to acquire.

Here's another example. In English, third person *-s* is a fairly simple notion, but it is late acquired by L2 learners of English universally—meaning it can take years for it to become part of the learner's representation and productive system, and only after other forms and features have been acquired. On the other hand, *-ing* to express progressive events (e.g., "I'm talking right now") is early acquired. One reason third person *-s* is difficult is the interface between syntax and phonology and phonetics. First, agreement has to be checked between verb and subject in the present tense, but then there is the issue of adding /s/ to consonants that end verbs. The verb *swim* for example is easy for L2 learners, but the final consonant cluster [mz] in *swims* is not as easy, as many languages prefer syllables that end in vowels. Worse still is something like *test*, where the third-person ending forms a cluster with three consonants: [sts] as in *tests*. In this case, you have an agreement rule that has to be acquired and its realization with the phonological system of English. *-ing*, on the other hand, has no agreement rule and is a simple combination of a vowel and a nasal sound, both of which are easily acquirable sounds and one of the easiest syllable structures universally: [iŋ]. (In spite of the fact that we spell it with *-ng*, there aren't two consonants in the actual pronunciation of *-ing*.)

Quick Reflection

Does the idea that some things are easy to acquire and some are difficult affect or influence what you think you *should* teach and/or what you think you *need* to teach?

These are just some of the issues that linguists and acquisitionists have looked at to account for easy/easier versus hard/harder things to acquire in a given language. By listing them, we don't mean to suggest they operate in isolation. In some cases, something can be difficult or later acquired for a variety of reasons—that is, some factors work together to make something more difficult than something else. In addition, there is the difference between acquisition of mental representation and the ability to deploy that representation while speaking. Something may exist in the mental representation of a learner but not make it out during the real-time act of speaking. What is more, we have focused on such things as inflections and syntax. There may be other factors to consider in the case of the sound system, for example, or pragmatics (speaker intent other than literal meaning), or even vocabulary (i.e., some words are easier to acquire than others). Finally, if the L1 has an influence on L2 acquisition, it would be in combination with the factors listed above and any others that scholars have examined. The idea that something is difficult in an L2 solely because it doesn't exist in the L1 or because it is somehow different from the L1 is too simplistic and inaccurate, according to the five decades of research we have. Again, each language has easy and hard things, as evidenced in both L1 and L2 acquisition.

Here are some readings if you'd like to delve into this topic more. A word of caution: Some of the readings may be very technical, so you may want to take your time with them!

Archibald, J. (2021, March). Ease and difficulty in L2 phonology: A mini-review. *Frontiers in Communication*. https://doi.org/10.3389/fcomm.2021.626529

Bulté, B., & Housen, A. (2012). Defining and operationalising L2 complexity. In A. Housen, F. Kuiken, & I. Vedder (Eds.), *Dimensions of L2 performance and proficiency: Complexity, accuracy and fluency in SLA* (pp. 21–46). John Benjamins.

DeKeyser, R. M. (2005). What makes learning second-language grammar difficult? *Language Learning*, *55*, 1–25.

Slabakova, R. (2013). What is easy and what is hard to acquire in a second language. In M. P. García Mayo, M. J. Gutierrez Mangado, & M. Martínez Adrián (Eds.), *Contemporary approaches to second language acquisition* (pp. 5–28). John Benjamins.

3. Aren't different parts of language learned differently?

As we discussed in Chapter 1, language is a complex phenomenon consisting of many moving parts that have to work together for the simplest of sentences to be produced or understood. The question on some teachers' minds is whether such things as vocabulary, grammar, and pronunciation are learned differently. The short answer is "No, not exactly." Let's see what we mean.

First, all components of language are acquired via what we covered in Chapter 3: Acquisition is input dependent and constrained by learners' internal mechanisms. This is true for vocabulary, grammar (the formal components for syntax and word formation and inflections), the sound system (including syllable structure), pragmatics (speaker intent), and so on. So, right away we see that the fundamental role of communicatively embedded input underlies all aspects of language.

As for internal mechanisms, Universal Grammar (UG) and language-specific mechanisms work on the formal components, while general learning mechanisms may work on other components. UG governs the nature of syntax and its interfaces with such things as morphology (word endings, prefixes, and so on) and phonology (the sound system), but it doesn't govern how words are learned—except for the interface that words have with the formal system. So, general learning mechanisms are responsible for helping us learn words and their meanings but not their underlying formal components. For example, *die* as a verb does not take an actor or agent as subject but what is called an experiencer. Dying is not an action, and no one actively does it. Dying is something an entity experiences. We can contrast it with the action of *speak* or *write*, which involves an active agent to bring it about. *Die* also only has one entity underlying its meaning (i.e., just the experiencer; there is no other entity that can or must be associated with the verb). This is why we can't "*die someone else" or "*die to someone else." In addition, as a verb, *die* has verb-related features, not noun-related features or determiner-related features. In short, the formal aspects of learning the verb *die* are governed by those mechanisms responsible for the formal components, while meaning and typical expressions with the verb (e.g., "die another day," "die on the vine," "die peacefully," "die laughing") and related uses are learned by general learning mechanisms. (*Note:* There is a field of linguistics called formal semantics that considers some aspects of meaning to be governed by universal features. A discussion of this field would take us far from the topic at hand.)

Quick Reflection

When teaching, how much attention do you pay to a word's formal properties, or do you only focus on meaning? Do you think there's a need to focus on formal properties, or do you assume their acquisition happens incidentally? Consider these words as well as any phrases or idioms that use them in the language you teach: *see, like, feel, worry, fall.*

This discussion brings to mind the following question: "What does it mean to know a word?" If we only think of words as things with meaning, we ignore the fact that words have grammatical properties. Let's look at one more example from Spanish: the verb *poner*. Learners are taught early on that this verb means "to put," as in *Russ pone la comida en la mesa* 'Russ is putting the food on the table.' Note that this use of *poner* requires three entities: the agent (i.e., the person/thing doing the putting), the object (i.e., the thing that is put), and the destination (i.e., where something is put). With any one of these items missing, the sentence would be ungrammatical. Later, learners might be taught that *poner* can be used with the reflexive pronoun *se* to mean "put on," like putting on an article of clothing: *Bill se pone los pantalones* 'Bill is putting on his pants.' But note what happens in the second use of *poner*: It loses the third entity involved in the first scenario (i.e., it loses its required destination). In the first one, Russ puts something somewhere. In the second, Bill doesn't put anything anywhere. To be sure, we can say Bill is in his room when he puts his pants on, but unlike the first instance of "put," the idea of a destination for putting something somewhere is gone (i.e., "in his room" is a location, not a destination). In fact, it's now impossible. Then, there is the use of *poner* with the pronoun *se* with verb phrases that loosely translate as "to begin doing something," as in *Bill se puso a cantar* 'Bill began to sing.' In this case, the verb *poner* again loses some of its original underlying entities. However, it also retains some underlying semantics in that whatever is the subject must be animate and capable of beginning something voluntarily or at least being actively involved in the event. This is why *La canoa se puso a hundirse* 'The canoe began to sink' sounds weird, if not awful, to speakers of Spanish, whereas *La canoa empezó a hundirse* (*empezó* 'began') sounds perfectly fine. *Poner* and *se* can also be used with certain adjectives that translate loosely into English: *become/turn/get* as in *Russ se puso rojo al oir eso* 'Russ turned/got red when hearing that.' However, not all adjectives fit with this phrase. For example, *Russ se puso independiente* 'Russ became independent' makes no sense to a Spanish speaker. Somehow, there is an underlying semantic restriction on the adjectives that can be used with this phrase (in this case, the action must be instantaneous, not something that occurs over time, and something out of the control of the entity undergoing the change). And notice once more that such a use disallows three entities compared to the base verb *poner* 'to put.' The point of this brief excursion into *poner* is that there is more to acquiring words than their typical meanings and there is an interaction between words and grammatical properties that leads to how words behave in sentences.

Many teachers are used to thinking that traditional vocabulary and grammar are learned differently—at least this is what we often hear in workshops and discussions. And textbooks, of course, separate vocabulary from grammar as though they are learned differently or unrelated. Teachers have been encouraged to explicitly test students on vocabulary and grammar separately on quizzes and exams. But textbook organization and what teachers are encouraged to do does not follow from the research on language and language acquisition since the 1970s. Vocabulary and the formal features of language go hand in hand, and both are input dependent during acquisition.

There are no readings we can recommend on this topic, as it has been largely ignored in L2 research. However, there are some resources where you can explore the interface between words and the formal properties of language, such as the journal *The Mental Lexicon*.

4. What about the first language? Doesn't it cause interference?

The role of the first language (L1) in second language (L2) acquisition is still debated in L2 research. Some scholars believe the L1 is the starting point for the L2. They claim that learners begin with something like an unconscious assumption that the L2 is just like the L1 until incoming data prove otherwise. In this scenario, everything in the L1 (except for words) is transferred into the L2 acquisition process. On the other end are those scholars who report no or minimal L1 influence in L2 acquisition. Their perspective is that learners begin L2 acquisition with some set of universals related to language and language processing that guide and shape development. Then there are other scholars who sit somewhere in the middle. From this perspective, L1 influence is "triggered" only when data from the input are processed in a way that causes the learning mechanisms to "think" that something in the L2 is just like something in the L1. We should underscore here that no matter the position scholars take, they agree that L1 influence happens without awareness. That is, like most aspects of acquisition, L1 influence involves unconscious or implicit processes during L2 acquisition.

Teachers are often surprised by the position that L1 influence may be constrained or minimal. They often report hearing their students produce sentences based on the L1. We hear French teachers talk about learners saying such things as *Je suis vingt ans* (literal meaning: "I am 20 years") as opposed to *J'ai vingt ans* (literal meaning: "I have 20 years") for "I am 20 years old." They point to what learners say as examples of L1 influence or transfer. However, in most cases, what teachers see is the result of a communication strategy: Learners generate a sentence in their L1 and "dress it up" in L2 words because they are pushed to communicate something beyond their capacity to do so. In other words, such utterances may be the result of task demands, not any acquisitional processes related to how the system actually develops over time. We will illustrate in the next paragraph what we mean by minimal L1 influence in acquisition.

Quick Reflection

Do you think teachers would see less L1 influence in learner production if learners weren't asked to speak in complete sentences from the outset or felt compelled to do so?

Remember the stages of acquisition from Chapter 2? In the acquisition of *ser* and *estar* in Spanish (the two verbs meaning something like "to be"), you might recall that the first stage in acquisition of these verbs is one in which no verb is used: *Russ alto* instead of *Russ es alto* for "Russ is tall" and

Bill no aquí instead of *Bill no está aquí* for "Bill isn't here." This is a curious stage if your language is English and you unconsciously assume that Spanish and English are the same. English does not allow the verb *be* to be deleted in such sentences—it has to appear in the sentence to carry tense (and in the present and past tense, some person-number information). So, "Russ tall" and "Bill not here" just aren't sentences in standard English. Learners of Spanish with English as their L1, then, don't seem to transfer the requirement for a verb like *be* to carry tense and person-number information. In fact, recent analyses suggest that at the earliest stage, learners don't seem to transfer the fact that English is a language that requires tense marking on verbs. Thus, it's a natural question to ask what happened to transfer or influence at the beginning. It doesn't seem to be there, at least in this and other documented phenomena.

This example is just one of many in the research on L2 acquisition in which L1 influence doesn't show up. To be sure, there are other examples in which L1 influence does seem to appear. This is particularly true of those working with linguistic theory in acquisition. Those working from a processing perspective seem split on the role of the L1 in how learners either comprehend or produce sentences. However, everyday experience with non-native speakers would suggest that L1 influence is often present in pronunciation—that is, we can often detect if someone has an accent. Interestingly, L1 influence is less prevalent in the mental representation of sounds. Research shows, for example, that learners can perceive sound differences even if they can't produce them.

We need to point out, however, that researchers look at L1 influence using techniques and methods of research that teachers don't use. Teachers tend to only see what their learners produce—and if learners are constantly pushed beyond their limits, they generally do wind up with a communication or production strategy of dressing an L1 sentence up in L2 words because they are compelled to, as we suggested earlier. In other words, what teachers often see learners do is prompted by the activities or tasks confronting them. The activity or task may push learners beyond their underlying representation, and when this happens, learners think in the L1, then translate those thoughts into the L2. But this is not transfer or L1 influence during acquisition itself. It is a task-induced strategy.

For the record, teachers are not the only ones who push learners beyond their current level of competence. Much of the research on L2 acquisition that demonstrates transfer does this as well. Research participants may be asked to do things that their underlying representation can't handle, so they rely on the language they know best to perform in the experiment or data-collection procedure. That language is their L1. Imagine, for example, that the learner is asked to judge whether this sentence in English is correct or not: "Bill reads often books by Chomsky." It probably sounds odd to you. But if you are a beginning learner of English with Spanish or French as your L1, how do you judge this sentence? You may not know enough English to judge it based on any underlying representation you've built up, so you translate it into your L1, and it sounds fine to you. You then check the box that says "This is a good sentence." (Spanish and French allow adverbs of manner and frequency to appear between verb and object; English doesn't. Example: *Bill lee a menudo libros de Chomsky/Bill lit souvant des livres de Chomsky.*) The researcher assumes this to be transfer. But we could equally view the response as a way to cope with a task that is beyond the learner's competence. To be sure, this isn't always the case with research. We are simply saying that researchers sometimes make assumptions about their research methods and what they represent that may or may not be valid for research on L1 influence.

For a variety of perspectives on the influence of the L1 in L2 acquisition, here are a few resources we recommend:

Andersen, R. W. (1983). Transfer to somewhere. In S. Gass & L. Selinker (Eds.), *Language transfer in language learning* (pp. 177–201). Newbury House.

Clahsen, H., & Felser, C. (2006). Grammatical processing in language learners. *Applied Psycholinguistics*, *27*, 3–42.

Pienemann, M. (2011). The psycholinguistic basis of PT. In M. Pienemann & J.-U. Kessler (Eds.), *Studying processability theory* (pp. 27–49). John Benjamins.

VanPatten, B. (2020). Input processing in adult L2 acquisition. In B. VanPatten, G. Keating, & S. Wulff (Eds.), *Theories in second language acquisition* (pp. 105–127). Routledge.

White, L. (2003). *Second language acquisition and universal grammar.* Cambridge University Press. (See especially Chapter 2 for a discussion of the initial state of L2 acquisition.)

5. What about errors? Don't learners develop bad habits if they aren't corrected?

Questions regarding errors are those that we perhaps hear the most from teachers. The main question is whether or not errors should be corrected. Common sense would suggest that errors should be corrected, because isn't that how we learn pretty much everything in life? We make a mistake, get corrected, and try not to do that thing again. But the assumption here is that language acquisition is like everything else. And that's a big assumption—in addition to the assumption that we actually learn from error correction in other domains of life. Here, though, we're interested in language, so that's our only focus.

We need to distinguish between what learners do in speaking with what they do in writing, especially if the latter involves composition and essay development. We'll see why in a minute. The research on correcting learners' oral production is not particularly robust, but what's there points to one conclusion: Error correction doesn't do much to aid acquisition. And this makes sense from a theoretical viewpoint. Let's recall the very basics of acquisition:

1. Learners need sustained access to comprehensible input in a communicative context.
2. Internal mechanisms related to language unconsciously work on processed input data over time so that a linguistic system evolves.

Given this most fundamental sketch, the question becomes "Where does error correction fit it?" It is not input, as we have defined it in this book or how it is defined in L2 research more generally. It is not part of the internal mechanisms, that's for sure. And if the internal mechanisms are designed to work on data from input, and error correction is not input, then what effect can such correction have? The answer is that the correction will have little effect because it just doesn't form the right "data set" for the internal mechanisms that unconsciously work on language (both Universal Grammar and general learning mechanisms, as described in Chapter 3). For the record, the small bit of research that hints at a role for error correction uses controlled tasks in which learners can easily monitor their output. That is, they can self-edit using conscious knowledge while speaking. But self-editing with conscious knowledge is not part of language acquisition. It is a skill separate from language acquisition itself—and not one that most learners are particularly good at in spontaneous communication, if we are honest.

To be clear, we mean error correction to be just what it sounds like: stopping someone and pointing out they did something wrong. However, there are indirect "corrections" that researchers have focused on that occur in conversations. Examples are clarification requests and recasts. Clarification requests involve someone asking learners if they meant something, as in this interchange:

Dave: Y yo, uh, yo fue temprano. 'And I, uh, I uh went (3rd sg) early.'

María: ¿Fuiste temprano? ¿O llegaste temprano? 'You went early or you arrived early?'

Dave: Oh, sí. Llegaste, I mean, llegó temprano. 'Oh, yes. You arrived, I mean, arrived (3rd sg) early.'

In this interchange, María queries whether Dave meant to say went early as in left early or arrived early. The clarification request pushes Dave to rethink what he said and how he said it, although the verbal inflection is non-native. Recasts, on the other hand, are simple restatements of what someone says, as in this interchange:

Dave: Y lo pasó bien. 'And he had a good time.'

María: Lo pasé bien. 'I had a good time.'

Dave: Sí, sí. Lo pasé bien. 'Yes, yes. I had a good time.'

Research on these kinds of interchanges with what we might call conversationally embedded feedback has yielded mixed results in terms of what they do. There was a flurry of this research in the 1980s and 1990s and somewhat into the early 2000s, but since then the research has dropped off in prominence, largely because scholars were not seeing it yielding much information on the extent to which such feedback actually affected anything. One of the problems in the research is showing impact on acquisition. In the example, when Dave says *Sí, sí. Lo pasé bien*, this is called *uptake*: The learner is showing immediate recognition of something. However, there is no research that actually shows longer-term or lasting impact of recasts and clarifications or that uptake (i.e., the learner immediately repeating something) affects acquisition. That is, in these laboratory studies and "in the wild" studies, there is no research on whether uptake has an impact 6 months or a year later; the research tends to look at the short-term gains only. Regardless of the mixed outcomes of this research, a reasonable takeaway for teachers would be this: Direct and explicit error correction seems to do little to help acquisition and impedes communication in the classroom. More indirect feedback mechanisms during interaction, such as recasts and clarification requests, are better suited for the communicative and proficiency-oriented classroom, even if we aren't sure to what extent they impact acquisition.

Quick Reflection

When learners produce something that is non-nativelike, what do you think that represents? Is the way you respond dependent on what you believe is the source of their non-nativelike production?

Now, what about writing and composition? In this domain, there is much more work on explicit error correction. However, the field is split. Some scholars claim it makes a difference. Some claim it doesn't. It's a complex area of research in which target structures, types of writing tasks, and determination about what an error is, among other factors, all make up part of a subfield of research that hasn't quite arrived at a consensus. For the moment, let's assume the research does suggest that error correction makes a difference in composition writing. This would make sense given what we said about self-editing earlier. It is in the written mode, with time and the motivation to self-correct (compositions are generally graded by teachers), where learners might be able to apply conscious knowledge about language in some way that masks what their true underlying (implicit) competence is. It is much harder to mask your competence with self-editing in spoken language. The takeaway here, however, is not so much that correction of written production affects the underlying system and how it grows; rather, it affects the conscious system and how it might get deployed in easily monitored writing.

Before moving on, we would like to ask you to consider the following: Would teachers be preoccupied with errors if they weren't called *errors*? What if they were called something like *non-nativelike structures* or *developmental structures*? We ask this because in our opinion, much of the concern about learner production comes from the use of the term *error* itself. Errors are bad things, right? They represent doing something wrong. A quick glance in *Roget's Thesaurus* finds some interesting synonyms for error: *blunder*, *delusion*, *fallacy*, *fault*, *sin*, and others. There's no getting around the fact that this particular term has negative connotations. Now, let's contrast the L2 situation with how people talk about child language. It's hard to find parents or adults who talk about a 2-year old's *errors*. We actually think such talk is cute ("Aww! Look what Phoebe just said!"). And the research in L1 acquisition is absolutely clear on the fact that parents just don't concern themselves with children's non-adultlike productions (until they get to school—and most of these non-adultlike productions involve word choice and a few highly infrequent things in the language). Parents largely ignore what children do and respond to the content: [Child] "Mommy. No soap!" [Parent] "Don't worry. I won't get soap in your eyes." Yet we stigmatize L2 learners by calling their non-nativelike productions *errors* (sins or blunders). Maybe that's something we need to think about as a profession. What might be a better term? How about *developmental productions*?

Here are some readings that will help you explore the topic further:

Leeman, J. (2007). Feedback in L2 learning: Responding to errors during practice. In R. M. DeKeyser (Ed.), *Practice in a second language: Perspectives from applied linguistics and cognitive psychology* (pp. 85–110). Cambridge University Press.

Li, S. (2010). The effectiveness of corrective feedback in SLA: A meta-analysis. *Language Learning*, *60*, 309–365.

VanPatten, B., Smith, M., & Benati, A. (2020). *Key questions in second language acquisition.* Cambridge University Press. (See particularly Chapter 3, "What Are the Roles of Input and Output?")

Williams, J. (2012). Classroom research. In S. M. Gass & A. Mackey (Eds.), *The Routledge handbook of second language acquisition* (pp. 541–554). Routledge.

6. Do the ACTFL Oral Proficiency Guidelines and Standards reflect ordered development?

This is an interesting question that we get from teachers from time to time. It reflects an attempt to connect ideas teachers encounter in different realms. Because ordered development refers to such things as sequences, stages, and so on, and the ACTFL guidelines refer to such things as levels and progression, the current question is a natural one. The answer, however, is that the guidelines don't reflect ordered development. The reverse is also true: Ordered development does not reflect proficiency as outlined in the ACTFL guidelines. To understand why, we will review both ideas here.

You may remember from Chapter 2 that ordered development refers to how *specific* linguistic features evolve over time in learners' mental representation. We find, for example, that when it comes to grammatical gender, there is always a gender that emerges as a default and is used before others. In the case of Spanish and French, masculine gender quickly emerges as the default, and feminine gender needs to be acquired over time. Something similar happens with plurality in languages that mark plurality. With both nouns and verb forms, singular emerges as the default and plural forms are the ones that need more time to be acquired. In languages with case systems, nominative case emerges as the default, and it is usually accusative that follows, although in complex case systems sometimes another that precedes the acquisition of accusative, as in the case of Russian. In short, ordered development is about linguistic feature X being acquired before feature Y or Z.

Also, with ordered development, we see stages in the acquisition of particular structures or features. In Chapter 2, we saw how the acquisition of *ser/estar* in Spanish evolves over time in four stages. We also saw summaries about staged development in negation, relative clauses, and other items. In short, ordered development is about linguistic features. What about proficiency levels?

Proficiency levels are not focused on linguistic features but instead on three things: what learners can talk about, the context in which they can talk about it, and how well they can talk about it. We can take the simple example of talking about one's family. At the novice level, learners can speak in short phrases or talk in listlike fashion with a lot of probing from the other interlocutor, while not providing much detail. The learner is largely dependent on the other person to co-construct the discourse (i.e., the learner tends to be reactive, not proactive). Here's an example:

> "My family? Oh, I, uh, I have two, uh, brothers. [Anyone else? No sisters?] No sisters. [What about your parents?] Oh, yes. My dad. My mom …"

At the intermediate level, learners would speak in more complete sentences and also string some of the sentences together with limited discourse connectors. They still tend to be reliant on the other person to co-construct the discourse, although there are signs of proactivity:

> "My family? I have a mom and dad. And I have two brothers. Uh, that's all. [That's all?] Well, I have a dog [laughs]."

At the advanced level, learners can speak in complete sentences and add information not normally offered at the previous levels as they expand on the topic and take more control of the conversation. By the time they reach the advanced level, learners are largely equally responsible for co-constructing discourse and have mostly left behind the dependency on the other person's work at moving the interaction along.

> "My family? Well, my mom and dad, they live in Sacramento. I have two brothers, both are older. One lives in Sacramento with his family and one lives in San Jose. My brother in San Jose isn't married. How about your family?"

Quick Reflection

In terms of your own teaching, which construct is more useful for (a) understanding acquisition, and (b) thinking about program assessment and outcomes? Ordered development or proficiency levels?

So, proficiency levels are about what learners can do with language in the context of an oral testing situation, with some implications about what they are able to do outside of the test. There is no reference to any particular structures or linguistic features. That is, there is no reference, for example, that at the novice level learners can use present tense and then at the intermediate level they can use simple past tense, or that at the novice level they use default gender and default number, with other gender and number features coming in at the intermediate level. The ACTFL Proficiency Guidelines were developed independently of research on ordered development and vice versa; ordered development of linguistic features and structures has been researched independently of proficiency as a construct. In addition, the ACTFL guidelines are not a description or explanation of acquisition. Technically, they are descriptors of performance at a particular point in time.

This does not mean that at some level some connections cannot be made. However, they just haven't been made yet. They are two independent strands of thinking about language development and communicative ability.

Unfortunately, there are no readings to which we can point for further discussion of this topic.

7. But isn't L2 acquisition different from L1 acquisition?

Most people don't know this, but L2 acquisition as a research field emerged in the late 1960s and early 1970s with the question of comparing L1 and L2 acquisition as directly as possible. The late 1950s and the 1960s were explosive decades for research on L1 acquisition, as was the 1970s for L2 acquisition. The early research argued for some fundamental similarities between L1 and L2 acquisition, and since then, there has been back-and-forth among scholars about these similarities. So, where are we today?

Borrowing from the epilogue of the 2020 book by Bill VanPatten, Megan Smith, and Alessandro Benati, there are two perspectives one can take, one internal and one external. By an internal perspective, we mean researching how language is processed and organized in the brain. By an external perspective, we mean researching factors not related to processing and organization of linguistic data. Let's take each in turn.

There is strong evidence that L1 and L2 acquisition involve fundamentally similar internal processes. Here are the basic facts:

- Both L1 and L2 acquisition require communicatively embedded input as the primary data for building a linguistic system.
- Both acquisitional contexts involve ordered and constrained development in much the same way (even if ordered development does not look exactly the same for L1 and L2 acquisition, although it often does).
- Neither L1 nor L2 acquisition seems amenable to outside manipulation (e.g., direct error correction or explicit learning and instruction).
- Both situations rely largely, if not exclusively, on implicit processing and learning.
- Both situations reveal individual rates of acquisition for learners.
- For both L1 and L2 acquisition, output is not a causal factor in the development of the linguistic system. In both cases, learner interactive output may encourage more and qualitatively different input over time.
- Even with an L1 present in the brain, the L2 learner shares all of the above with the L1 learner. The presence of an L1 does not seem to change the fundamental processes or mechanisms involved in L2 acquisition as stated in the previous points, for example. It may simply gum up the works or, in some cases, push the processes along. But it does not alter the underlying processes.

At the same time, there is evidence that L1 and L2 acquisition show important external differences. Here are a few:

- Disposition seems to affect L2 acquisition but not the fundamental mechanisms or processes. It seems to affect how far learners get and the degree to which they want to be "nativelike." Motivation is not a significant factor in L1 acquisition in terms of rate or how far learners get. All toddlers seem to want to learn language and do.
- Communicatively embedded input is more varied across L2 learners and may not be as plentiful as it is for L1 learners. By the time a child reaches school age, that child has amassed more than 13,000 hours of interaction with input and with other speakers in communicative settings in the L1.

Unless an L2 learner is living and working abroad and has completely shut himself or herself off from any L1 contact, it would take years for a learner to amass the same quantity and quality of interaction with input.

- Social contexts differ for children and adults. Children are allowed to be children. Except for using good behavior (e.g., "Don't be mean"; "Play nice"; "Say 'please'"), children are allowed to be children, and we engage them in language at their level of cognitive development (e.g., coloring, telling fairy tales, playing with puppets). We expect and allow them to speak in one- and two-word utterances, for example. Adults are expected to be adults. Society expects them to engage in adult topics and events, not childlike events. We expect adults to speak in intelligible sentences. (See the discussion on errors elsewhere in these FAQs and how expectations seem to affect how differently we view child L1 production versus adult L2 production.) And because they're adults, there are often expectations that they acquire languages differently from children, which in turn affects a variety of factors related to acquisition.
- Teenagers and adults may place demands on themselves that preschool L1 children do not (e.g., "I need to sound intelligent"; "I don't want to make mistakes"; "They are going to judge me, so I'd better be good at this").

From these brief and not all-inclusive lists, the answer to whether L1 and L2 acquisition are the same or different depends on whether you are looking at the linguistic and psycholinguistic aspects of acquisition or at the external nonlinguistic aspects. From our reading of the research from the past 50 years, L1 and L2 acquisition are fundamentally similar at their core. What happens inside the human mind does not vary much depending on context. But powerful external or nonlinguistic forces may shape the extent to which L2 learners progress and move toward nativelike mental representation and ability—and task demands may push them to do things such as rely on the L1 to generate utterances (see the FAQ on the influence of the L1).

Quick Reflection

How does the external reality of teaching impact your (a) decision-making and (b) what you expect of learners?

An influential essay on the L1/L2 topic was published by Robert Bley-Vroman in 1989. In that essay, he launched the Fundamental Difference Hypothesis—and many scholars and teachers point to this essay as a basis for claiming that L1 and L2 acquisition are different. His central claim was that L1 children are guided by Universal Grammar during acquisition, but adult L2 learners are not. Instead, they rely on general learning mechanisms or problem-solving skills. Unfortunately for the hypothesis, this fundamental claim has not received strong support in the literature. In fact, there is abundant evidence that L2 acquisition is guided by Universal Grammar. The prevailing hypothesis today is called Full Access, meaning that despite other differences, L2 learners have full access to the contents of Universal Grammar and that child L1 and adult L2 learners, for example, are exploiting similar processes at their core to create a linguistic system. Bonnie Schwartz and Rex Sprouse are scholars who repeatedly show this process, and we have provided readings on the topic in this section. Outside the framework of linguistic theory, scholars in other frameworks concur that the underlying processes in L1 and L2 acquisition are similar (e.g., usage-based approaches), so the idea of a fundamental difference is also questioned, if not outright rejected.

With the above said, sometimes we hear "Yes, but the research shows that child and adult brains are different. Therefore, learning should be different for the two populations." Although there are some differences between child and adult brains, when it comes to acquisition, brain difference has no impact. It does have an impact on how people *learn* explicitly, but it doesn't affect how people *acquire* language or process the environment implicitly. The same underlying mechanisms are involved in both contexts. This is the conclusion of scholars from a variety of perspectives: linguistic theory, usage-based approaches, functional approaches, and processing approaches. In particular, research using a technique called Event-related Potentials (ERPs), which measures brain activity, has increasingly shown how quickly L2 learners' neural patterns resemble those of native speakers for learners with non-impaired cognitive ability.

As one final point, you may have heard of the Critical Period Hypothesis (CPH), which was developed for L1 acquisition back in the 1960s and claimed that if you did not learn a first language by a certain age, you couldn't learn language. It was not a claim about L2 acquisition. However, some L2 scholars subsequently took it to mean that you couldn't learn any language after a certain age—L1, L2, or another language. Much research time was spent on the CPH until the late 1990s, and the growing consensus is that there is no CPH, but there is an age issue. Because language acquisition takes so long and L1 speakers already have a well-worn processing mechanism for one language, this has led researchers to think that the issue is not a critical period issue. Instead, adults just have baggage that gets in the way. This doesn't make L2 acquisition different from L1 acquisition in terms of mechanisms or processes, just typically more difficult.

Understanding both the internal similarities and the external differences between L1 and L2 acquisition can help teachers make determinations about whether or not to explicitly teach grammar, argue for approaches in the classroom that emphasize input and interaction (for example), and consider how to do so in a socially appropriate way for teenagers and adults.

Here are some publications that will help you explore this topic in more detail:

Bley-Vroman, R. (1989). What is the logical problem of foreign language learning? In S. Gass & J. Schachter (Eds.), *Linguistic perspectives on second language acquisition* (pp. 41–68). Cambridge University Press.

Chenu, F., & Jisa, H. (2009). Reviewing some similarities and differences in L1 and L2 lexical development. *Acquisition et Interaction en Langue Étrangère, Aile...Lia 1*, 17–38.

Herschensohn, J. (2007). *Language development and age.* Cambridge University Press.

Schwartz, B., & Sprouse, R. (2013). Generative approaches and the poverty of the stimulus. In J. Herschensohn & M. Young-Scholten (Eds.), *The Cambridge handbook of second language acquisition* (pp. 137–158). Cambridge University Press.

VanPatten, B., Smith, M., & Benati, A. (2020). *Key questions in second language acquisition.* Cambridge University Press. (See the epilogue in particular.)

8. Don't learners have to speak to learn a language?

It's a prevailing belief among both practitioners and the public that speaking is required to learn a language. We believe this belief stems largely from two sources. First, many believe that language learning involves consciously learning something (e.g., a rule, a sound, a word), then applying it in some way—that is, practicing it via some kind of oral production. To put this in other words, the idea is that learners move from explicit knowledge to implicit knowledge via some kind of speaking practice (see Chapter 4 for more on this). And second, speaking is seen as the primary reason to learn a language. Most people don't learn a language because they want to read newspapers or watch television from another country. They engage in language learning so they can speak and carry on conversations. If speaking is the goal, then it should be the path by which we learn languages, so to speak (no pun intended!).

Both of these beliefs were, perhaps unintentionally, encouraged by the development of the ACTFL Oral Proficiency Guidelines in the 1980s, along with the push to measure oral proficiency. Many methodologists at the time (and maybe some still) used the concept of oral proficiency as a goal to underscore the need to explicitly learn grammar and vocabulary, followed by speaking practice of some kind. Indeed, this is the prevailing belief underlying almost all current commercial language textbooks in the United States for grades 6 through 12 and university-level courses. Around the same time, something called the Output Hypothesis was developed, which, in its original form, claimed that learning to speak was a process independent of language acquisition itself. Thus, according to the Output Hypothesis, learners needed not only abundant access to input but also opportunities for the expressive side of communication.

As we've discussed in various places in this book, speaking is not required for developing a mental representation of language. As outlined in Chapter 3, the essential ingredients are communicatively embedded input from the environment and internal acquisition mechanisms. These are the only *necessary* ingredients for acquisition of language as mental representation. In Chapter 3, we touched on the role of interaction (when learners engage with other speakers) to discuss how it might be beneficial, but not necessary, for the acquisition of language itself. As research as far back as

1978 has shown, interaction provides learners with better input than canned input or input that is part of "talking at" learners.

Quick Reflection

Have you considered your own teaching and the difference between *making* learners talk and *providing opportunities* so that they want to talk?

There is one framework sometimes used to talk about acquisition that is explicit about the role of "speaking as practice": skill theory. Under this theory, the skill of speaking must be practiced, and learners move from learned material (e.g., textbook grammar and vocabulary) to productive ability with that material. The problem with this approach, as many have pointed out, is that it cannot account for the complex, rich, and implicit linguistic system that learners develop—a system that underlies ability with language. What is more, research supporting the need for speaking practice suffers from the limitations of other kinds of laboratory studies: The research only looks at short-term gains after a brief practice period. As we discussed in Chapter 4, other areas of research have shown that short-term gains wear off and usually disappear. The research also tends to focus on one thing at time, yet we know that in language acquisition, learners are working on multiple aspects of language at once. It becomes difficult, then, to translate these focused laboratory studies into something as complex as acquisition.

But mental representation is one thing. What about communicative language ability, especially expressive ability? If communication is the expression and interpretation of meaning in a given context for a given purpose, how do learners develop the ability to express meaning? First, expressive ability assumes some kind of mental representation; learners have to tap something in order to produce language. That representation need not be complete or nativelike for learners to engage in spontaneous communication, much as a 2-year-old may engage in communication with parents and siblings without having a full-fledged mental representation of language. So, some kind of mental representation almost always precedes the ability to communicate (using that representation), no matter the stage of acquisition in which learners find themselves—although in the earliest stages of acquisition, non-child learners can use some explicit knowledge about language to communicate, albeit roughly and often not well, as their implicit mental representation develops. The ability to use explicit knowledge during communication breaks down easily with pressure in real time.

Quick Reflection

In L1 acquisition, children are expected to speak in one- and two-word utterances. Adults understand that this is what children can do. No one asks a 2-year-old to speak in complete sentences. What expectations do you have for L2 learners in terms of their productive abilities when they are starting out? On what do you base these expectations?

What is more, communication is context dependent. Learners must not only acquire language itself—they must also acquire the rules of engagement, as it were, including what to say and how best to say it in the context in which one is communicating. These rules address when not to talk, as well as how to interrupt or take a turn, strategize, let others know their meaning was correctly interpreted, show deference with language, and choose words and phrases carefully depending on context (i.e., the participants and setting). In short, communication goes beyond mental representation of language itself. The question, then, is not so much whether speaking is necessary for language acquisition (it isn't), but whether speaking is necessary in order to learn how to participate in conversations. This is a very good question that is hardly ever asked, and it is largely ignored in research, if it is researched at all.

In L1 acquisition, for example, little kids develop a mental representation for language based on the input they are exposed to along with internal learning mechanisms. But they learn how to "behave" with language by engaging in conversations. "Say 'thank you'"; "Shhh. Don't interrupt"; and "We don't use that word, honey" are examples of what little kids receive as explicit communication feedback during conversations, regardless of their level of language. We don't know if such feedback is required to develop communicative ability, but we do know it is present. Assuming such feedback is useful, if not necessary, to develop expressive communicative ability in L1 context-dependent situations, it would reasonable to conclude that such feedback is also useful—if not necessary—in L2 situations.

Thus, speaking is not necessary for acquiring language, but it may be necessary for learning how to behave with language. In this scenario, once again the distinction between language and communication (see Chapter 1) is important for addressing a fundamental belief among practitioners and the public. We like the following quote from famed anthropologist Margaret Mead that is somewhat illustrative of what we mean:

> "I am not a good mimic and I have worked now in many different cultures. I am a very poor speaker of any language, but I always know whose pig is dead, and when I work in a native society, I know what people are talking about and I treat it seriously and I respect them, and this in itself establishes a great deal more rapport, very often, than the correct accent. I have worked with other field workers who were far, far better linguists than I, and the natives kept on saying they couldn't speak the language, although they said I could! … You see, you don't need to teach people to speak like natives, you to make the other people believe they can, so they can talk to them, and then they learn."

While Mead's comments reflect her own experience, others would concur. The idea here is that as teachers understand the difference between acquiring language and learning how to communicate, they will be better able to reflect on what to teach, how to teach it, and to what extent any kind of explicit teaching is necessary.

Here are some classic readings, along with several overviews, for you to explore the topic further:

Day, R. (Ed.). (1986). *Talking to learn: Conversation in second language acquisition*. Newbury House.

Derwing, T. M., Munro, M. J., & Thomson, R. I. (Eds.). (2022). *The Routledge handbook of second language acquisition and speaking*. Routledge.

Hawkins, R. (2019). *How second languages are learned: An introduction.* Cambridge University Press. (See especially Chapter 9, in which he discusses the role of output in acquisition.)

Mackey, A. (2007). Interaction as practice. In R. M. DeKeyser (Ed.), *Practice in a second language: Perspectives from applied linguistics and cognitive psychology* (pp. 85–110). Cambridge University Press.

Savignon, S. (1995). *Communicative competence: Theory and classroom practice*. McGraw-Hill.

9. Doesn't everything come down to motivation?

Although we touched on motivation as part of disposition in Chapter 3, we will add to the discussion here.

Motivation is a factor in many aspects of our lives. Motivation is involved in finishing projects (like this book), finding a new job or starting a new career, and, of course, dieting and exercising. Motivation appears to be key in how successful we are in doing something or how far we get—and even whether or not we start something. So, when we hear the question "Doesn't everything come down to motivation?" the answer is "Not exactly." Here's why we answer that way.

In L2 acquisition, motivation is clearly implicated in the following decisions:

- whether or not we start learning another language
- whether we seek out opportunities for input and interaction with that input (e.g., see Chapter 3)
- how often and to what extent we seek out those opportunities (e.g., every day, twice a week, with different people or only one person—although see the FAQ on social factors)

Motivation is not implicated in the following processes:

- ordered development and how acquisition unfolds over time (e.g., see Chapter 2)
- the implicit workings of language acquisition (e.g., see Chapters 1 and 4)

And because motivation isn't implicated in those processes, it is not a factor in how the internal mechanisms responsible for language acquisition work (see Chapter 3 on internal ingredients). That is, whether we are motivated or not, and no matter how strong our motivation, we have no control over the unconscious internal processes that guide and shape acquisition. Let's take the case of dieting. Motivation keeps us on the diet, but it has no control over our metabolism. Motivation keeps us on the diet, but it has no control over the number of calories a body needs as opposed to what the body expends or even what kinds of calories are best. Motivation keeps us on a diet, but it doesn't indicate what kind of exercise is best for us or exactly how to do that exercise. In short, motivation may be the *why* for many things we do, but it doesn't help us with the *how*.

Quick Reflection

What motivated you to become a proficient speaker of another language? Do your students have the same motivation? If not, what implications do you think there are for the classroom?

In L2 research, scholars have focused on different aspects of motivation—and in fact, over time, there have been shifts in theoretical stances on motivation. For example, early in the 1950s and up until the 1990s, a social-psychological perspective was at the core of motivation research. Much of this research was based on the Canadian experience in which two official languages co-existed and researchers were interested in such things as integration (e.g., wishing to belong to the other culture) versus instrumental motivation (e.g., using language for utilitarian purposes). Other trends have dominated the field over the years, and currently there seems to be an emphasis on what can be called *socio-dynamic issues*. This emphasis has a concern for the conditions under which interactions happen and is more closely tied to a focus on social factors in L2 acquisition. No matter the theoretical position or period of research, the focus has been on the *why* of acquisition and the *how* of learners seeking interactions or opportunities. It has not focused on the *how* of development itself.

So, motivation may be "everything" when it comes to whether we even try to acquire a language, but it has nothing to do with how language evolves in our head over time. With this said, teachers are often concerned about motivation in their captive audience—also known as students. They constantly seek ways to motivate their students. There is no magic wand for motivating students, but there is some common sense involved. Classrooms in which abundant amounts of input embedded in communicative events involving compelling and engaging topics and themes are more motivating than classrooms that don't provide such things. Each teacher has to find his or her way to provide such an environment. Exclusive reliance on typical textbooks may stifle teachers' search for such environments.

Interestingly, and perhaps paradoxically, nothing is more motivating than success. That is, when someone feels a sense of accomplishment, that person is more likely to be motivated to continue doing something that brought about that sense of accomplishment. Thus, another avenue for teachers to pursue, if their goal is language acquisition for their learners, is providing clear indicators of what has been accomplished along the way and building success into the curriculum. This is no easy task in a language acquisition environment, but doing an internet search and discussing with colleagues who are involved in acquisition-rich, input-based classrooms will lead teachers to find alternatives to tests and feedback that will help learners see what they can do and be proud of it. Zoltán Dörnyei, a leading scholar in motivation research, published a set of strategies for helping motivation along in a classroom. You will find that reference below, along with one recent overview that should prove useful for understanding the focus of motivation research.

Dörnyei, Z. (2001). *Motivational strategies in the language classroom.* Cambridge University Press.

Ushioda, E., & Dörnyei, Z. (2015). Motivation. In S. M. Gass & A. Mackey (Eds.), *The Routledge handbook of second language acquisition* (pp. 396–409). Routledge.

10. What about individual differences and different learning styles?

In educational circles, individual differences and learning styles are important. As the saying goes, not everyone learns the same way—and this concept is applied to the education of math, the sciences, the social sciences, and other areas to accommodate students' individual differences or needs. Individual differences include everything from motivation to working memory (we touched on those particular differences in Chapter 3), while learning styles include everything from the tolerance of ambiguity to whether or not people feel the need to write things down. But what roles do such differences play in language acquisition?

There are two ways of looking at this question. The first is that when it comes to language itself, individual differences and learning styles do not exert any influence on how language evolves in someone's head over time (Chapters 2 and 4). For example, whether or not you tolerate ambiguity matters little in the acquisition of plural markers in a language like Spanish. These always come after the acquisition of singular markers. The acquisition of third person *-s* in English comes much later than the acquisition of past tense marking on verbs whether you are male or female, left-brain oriented or right-brain oriented, or whether or not you like to take notes. That nominative case is acquired before accusative case in languages like German and Russian has little to do with learning styles. That passive structures are acquired later than active structures in languages like English and Turkish is unrelated to working memory differences in individuals. In short, language acquisition is on a learner's internal timetable, independent of personal motivation, individual differences, and learning styles. This has been shown time and time again in the research on a variety of languages across lots of populations.

The other way to look at the question is about how learners engage input and how they seek it out. As we've discussed in this book, language acquisition is input dependent—and input is defined as communicatively embedded language that learners hear or see. It is language they attempt to comprehend as part of some communicative event, whether during a conversation, while reading, while chatting online, or while watching television. Do individual differences affect how learners engage with input in some way? Surprisingly, there is little research, if any, on this topic, but there are some commonsense ways for us to view the situation. Let's look at extroversion and introversion as one possible type of difference.

Extroverts seek company, like interacting with others, and may even enjoy being at the center of attention. Introverts ... much less so. It could be, then, that extroverts are better at interacting with others and seeking opportunities for more exposure to language (i.e., communicatively embedded input). If so, they might progress faster in acquisition and even communicative ability (see FAQ on the role of speaking). Not only might they get more input, but it will be input in which they have a higher stake because of their involvement. In this scenario, the extrovert/introvert difference could affect both quantity and quality of input that learners receive. We are, of course, speculating. It could be that introverts find their own ways to interact with language that don't involve "public displays of behavior." But the idea is that personality differences may affect the rate of acquisition because of how learners choose to engage input, with whom they do it, and what kind of input they engage.

Quick Reflection

You have two students, Ricky and Elena. Elena is an extrovert and a chatterbox. Ricky is an introvert and tends to be quiet. Do you respect those differences, or do you force Ricky to talk more in class?

Another example of an individual difference is the tolerance of ambiguity. People fall on a scale of comfort with tolerating things they don't quite grasp or don't quite fully understand. How might this impact acquisition? Again, individual differences in this regard don't affect how language evolves in the head over time, but, again, they may affect how learners engage input. We can imagine a scenario in which those who tolerate ambiguity plow ahead while listening or reading, perhaps thinking something like "I'll get what she's saying eventually," while others with less tolerance might bristle or even give up because they want to understand every word they hear or see but can't. Which learner is more likely to keep engaging with communicatively embedded input and thus get more exposure over time? Again, such questions are under-researched—if they are researched at all—but they seem important for us to understand how to deal with the way in which classroom learners might handle input and interaction with that input.

As we see it, then, the bottom line with individual differences is that they do not directly or even indirectly affect the time-course of development of language in a learner's head. Language unfolds in particular ways over time independently of learner differences. However, we envision scenarios in which certain individual differences may affect how learners seek out input, what kind of input they seek, and how they engage the input. Such differences may impact acquisition at the macro level—that is, how far and how quickly learners acquire language and the ability to communicate with it.

Note that we focus here on the acquisition of language. However, the explicit learning of aspects of language found in many classrooms may be affected by individual differences such as learning styles. But as we have seen elsewhere in this book, the link between explicit learning and acquisition is weak, at best (e.g., Chapter 4).

An excellent and readable overview of individual differences and personality factors related to acquisition can be found in the following chapter:

Dewaele, J.-M. (2013). Learner-internal psychological factors. In J. Herschensohn & M. Young-Scholten (Eds.), *The Cambridge handbook of second language acquisition* (pp. 159–179). Cambridge University Press.

11. Don't imitation and repetition play a role in acquisition?

The idea that language acquisition somehow involves the imitation of what other speakers do was an idea that predominated the pre-empirical days of both L1 and L2 research. It stems from theories of behaviorism that dominated psychology in the early and mid-20th century. Behaviorists believed that child L1 acquisition was a matter of (in the simplest of terms) children's attempts to imitate adults, then getting rewarded for the imitation. This basic idea was transferred into L2 learning and formed the basis for audiolingual methodology—an approach to teaching that emphasized dialogue memorization and particular kinds of drills in which students imitated or repeated what the teacher said. Free communication was avoided until learners had "mastered the patterns."

The research on both L1 and L2 acquisition that blossomed in the 1960s and 1970s swiftly put an end to any significant role for imitation and repetition as acquisitional processes. As should be evident from other parts of this book, language acquisition for everyone (both L1 and L2, in all contexts, including classroom and non-classroom) turned out to be something we might call *creative construction*. Learners pick up bits and pieces of language from what they are exposed to, and these bits and pieces are used by internal devices to slowly construct a linguistic system over time (see especially Chapters 2 and 4). Nothing that L1 children or L2 learners do ever really resembles the results of imitation.

In spite of the research, the idea that imitation somehow plays an important role in L2 acquisition lingers. In pop culture (e.g., movies, television), it is not uncommon to see adults trying to learn languages by imitating a recording or by repeating what a teacher says. Indeed, some popular non-academic learning platforms make ample use of imitation and repetition. This is just another example of how the science says one thing, but belief leads people to follow a different course.

Quick Reflection

Do imitation and repetition play a part in your language teaching? If so, where did this practice come from? How did you learn to do it?

With all of this said, it is not out of the question that someone could repeat and memorize some basic phrases and even sentences to prepare for a trip or some kind of encounter with speakers of another language. However, what that person is doing involves memorizing whole chunks of language, not actually creating any linguistic system in his or her head. Such memorization could be useful for specific purposes or functions under restricted conditions, but we should not confuse it with acquisition itself (i.e., evolution of a mental representation that can be used to generate novel utterances). To make this concrete, anyone can memorize the question "Where is the bathroom?" for the purpose of traveling, but the memorization of that one sentence does not imply that the person has acquired *wh-* movement (i.e., *where* has moved from its original part of the sentence to another part in other to make a question); that tense is required (i.e., the copular verb *be* is necessary to indicate present tense); or, for example, that a definite article is required to indicate such things as specificity, definiteness, and assumed existence (i.e., *the bathroom* as opposed to *a bathroom* or *bathroom*).

One reason that imitation and repetition might still be considered by many teachers to be a viable practice in class is that they provide the *illusion* of learning or acquisition. If, for example, a learner can repeat something a teacher says, then it *appears* that something is happening. Because teachers can't observe what goes on in learners' minds as they interact with communicatively embedded input, they may wish to have learners do something observable (even if it is not clear what that observed thing is or if it contributes to learning). Another reason may be that teachers (and perhaps learners) believe that imitation and repetition are how we learn more generally. We memorize a name by repeating it to ourselves several times. We mimic recipes by watching someone on television and imitating what the person does. Actors rehearse and repeat lines to prepare for a play or a scene. We could find examples like these in everyday life. If imitation and repetition are assumed to be part of learning more generally, then why not for language, too? The problem with this idea is that in such situations, language is *the medium for* imitation and repetition of names, lines, recipes, and so on. Language is not *the object of* imitation and repetition in everyday life. It is not the outcome. It is a tool.

You can read just about any book on child L1 acquisition to understand why imitation and repetition are not the foundations for learning. Likewise, in just about any book on L2 acquisition, you will find imitation and repetition to be absent as foundations for learning. Here are readings covering both of these topics:

Hawkins, R. (2019). *How second languages are learned.* Cambridge University Press.

Herschensohn, J., & Young-Scholten, M. (Eds.). (2013). *The Cambridge handbook of second language acquisition.* Cambridge University Press.

Lightbown, P., & Spada, N. (2021). *How languages are learned.* 5th ed. Oxford University Press.

Lust, B. (2006). *Child language: Acquisition and growth.* Cambridge University Press.

Rowland, C. (2014). *Understanding child language acquisition.* Routledge.

VanPatten, B., Keating, G. D., & Wulff, S. (Eds.). (2020). *Theories in second language acquisition.* Routledge.

12. Doesn't giving learners rules help? (That's the way I learned ...)

Instructors will often tell us that they learned a particular way, and based on their experience, they believe that is how language acquisition happens. When we look beneath the surface of such claims, we find several interesting things. The first is that memory is selective. The second is that the belief doesn't jive with research. Let's talk about selective memory first.

Those of us who experienced any kind of classroom learning may very well remember reading textbooks, getting rules, practicing, and so on. We might even remember particular episodes in those classes. For example, Bill VanPatten remembers his French teacher in high school saying, "*J'aime beaucoup les bonbons*," along with the face she made as she talked about liking chocolate candies. It is not an uncommon experience to have such memories. But what we generally fail to remember is what happened to us after those early classroom experiences. Here's the question: If we are advanced or superior speakers or knowers of a language, did we get to that level because of our first 2 years of language classes? Or is there something else that is common to our experiences? What instructors who are near-native speakers of another language tend not to recall are all of the experiences they had outside of those early days of the classroom. Very advanced learners have received tremendous amounts of input and interaction. They've read. They've lived abroad. They've watched movies. They've immersed themselves in a culture. Perhaps they married a speaker of that language. And most important, they've had the disposition to stick with the long-haul nature of acquisition. In Bill's case, he's reflected on experiences outside of language classes and all the things he did to actually learn French: He hung around French speakers in grad school, found movies he liked and watched them repeatedly, went to France for a summer, and taught in Quebec another summer, among other things. The point is that when he thinks about the totality of his experiences and is honest with how French has gotten in his head, it's because of the things he did outside the classroom. In fact, Bill will admit he doesn't remember much about textbooks and activities in class, and most of his knowledge of French comes from intuition and what feels right to him. When advanced speakers of another language are pushed to reflect, their experiences tend to resemble Bill's.

So, from our perspective of experience, the question is not "Doesn't giving learners rules help?" but instead "Aren't all the other things we do to acquire language more important or fundamental?" What this suggests is that if we reflect carefully, no matter what we think of what we learned in classes, our advanced ability with language must include our accumulated experiences outside classes. In fact, we should give a good deal of weight to such experiences. Our point is that relying on what we remember is only useful if we remember *everything* that ever happened to us. We need to be aware of selective memory and its seductive power to reduce acquisition to something simple.

Quick Reflection

Are you comfortable with learners developing intuitions? Or do you feel the need for them to "know" rules and be able to state them? Which is more important for developing advanced proficiency?

With that said, some instructors might claim that giving rules early on provides a foundation for acquisition. This is where we go to our second point: what the research says. In various chapters in this book, we have discussed the basic findings of the effects of explicit instruction. The general conclusion from such research is that explicit instruction (including learning rules) results in explicit knowledge. We touched on this in Chapter 4. There is no evidence that it affects the abstract, complex, and implicit mental representation we call language—and, as we have argued, explicit knowledge doesn't turn into implicit knowledge. When we say there is no evidence, we mean precisely that: There is no evidence. There is conjecture, as researchers sometimes make arguments that go beyond what the research data actually say. However, conjecture is not evidence. If research on language acquisition is to have any scientific validity or to provide any insights to instructors, scholars must stick to the facts. They cannot engage in "yes, but" when their data don't offer evidence that they (or others) don't want to hear.

Let's take a simple example regarding three structures in Spanish, researched by Bill VanPatten, Gregory D. Keating, and Michael Leeser in 2012. They looked at learners who were in the intermediate stage of Spanish, taking classes at the third-year level at the university. They compared these learners to native speakers and looked at how the participants performed on an online, self-paced reading task in which they read grammatical and ungrammatical sentences. (In self-paced reading, participants read sentences either word by word or in short phrases on a computer, advancing through the sentence by pushing a button. This procedure forces them to keep things in working memory and build sentence structure in their heads as they move along the sentence without the ability to look back.) What the researchers found was that the learners patterned like native speakers on two structures that were not taught: sentence structure for questions and adverb placement with a rare construction. The learners demonstrated unconscious reaction to ungrammatical sentences by longer reading times at key points. However, on the very thing that learners were taught and presumably practiced from the earliest stages—subject-verb agreement—the learners did not pattern like native speakers. They did not show any unconscious reaction to ungrammatical sentences, and their reading times were the same for grammatical and ungrammatical sentences. They didn't slow down at key points like native speakers. This was particularly surprising because the subjects and verbs were next to each other in each sentence they read. What this study showed is that learners had implicit knowledge they used when processing two structures but did not have the same kind of implicit knowledge when processing another structure.

The VanPatten, Keating, and Leeser study was not about instruction, but the results are useful for discussion here. Learners clearly were not building a mental representation involving subject-verb agreement after years of practice with verb forms or they would have patterned like native speakers. After all, they did pattern like natives on the other structures that weren't taught. The results of this research are corroborated by other scholars' research on how subject-verb development happens over time with learners, such as that by Corrine McCarthy. In short, the explicit instruction and explicit practice with verb forms just doesn't seem to do much for acquisition. Like most aspects of language, learners slowly build a representation for such things as they engage with input in communicative contexts over time.

Returning, then, to the issue of saying, "That's the way I learned," it can't be claimed that providing rules and practicing them provides some kind of foundation. There is no evidence that such activity is beneficial and no evidence that it is necessary. Yet we find that this is the most difficult belief for instructors to overcome, so powerful is their belief in what they think happened to them that 50 years of accumulated research does not convince them otherwise.

There is no research directly related to the question at hand, but a general reading of the L2 acquisition research from more than 50 years would lead to the claims made here. Here are two references for the studies mentioned in this FAQ:

McCarthy, C. (2012). Modeling morphological variation and development: Person and number in L2 Spanish. *Linguistic Approaches to Bilingualism*, *2*(1), 25–53.

VanPatten, B., Keating, G. D., & Leeser, M. J. (2012). Missing verbal inflections as a representational issue: Evidence from on-line methodology. *Linguistic Approaches to Bilingualism*, *2*, 109–140.

13. What about social factors? Don't they affect acquisition in a significant way?

In the early 2000s, much was made about social factors in L2 research. The basic idea was there was too much emphasis on the linguistic and cognitive aspects in scholarship and not enough about the learner in a social context or as a social being. Scholars such as Dwight Atkinson, Bonny Norton, and David Block emerged as voices in the field along with others. Constructs such as learner identity, socialization, contexts and setting, and learner agency formed the core of discussion. The question for us is this: Given that social factors are important, *how* are they important?

We begin by saying that in terms of explaining such things as ordered development, how language is organized in the mind, and constraints on acquisition that we have discussed in this book, social factors do not play a significant role. That is, there is nothing about social factors such as learner identity or agency that explains or has an effect on staged development or how language evolves as mental representation. That learners tend to learn one thing earlier than another (e.g., singular before plural, masculine before feminine) or that the acquisition of something like copular verbs in Spanish or negation in English involves stages over time is not affected by social factors. Keep in mind that much of what we know about the evolution of mental representation of language and of language processing by learners has been researched in all kinds of contexts with all kinds of learners from various languages and ages. With such a rich data set from more than 50 years of research, it is safe to say that social factors do not play a role in the cognitive or linguistic aspects of acquisition. So, why are social factors important, then, and why have some scholars turned their attention to this area of research?

Our perspective is that although social factors are not important in terms of acquisition of language, they are critical to understanding how communication or interaction develops, as well as why learners continue with acquisition, abandon it, or decide what they can do is good enough. And, of course, these factors are important when one is concerned with a learner's integration into another culture or setting. In this sense, social factors play roles similar to those mentioned in Chapter 3 (e.g., disposition). Let's look at the following example.

Learner agency refers to how people in L2 social contexts make (informed) choices or exert influence over what happens to them. This can include resisting something (e.g., being forced to speak) or complying with something (e.g., going with the flow). As a concrete example, Bill VanPatten recalls one time at a dinner party in Quebec where everyone spoke French. Three were native speakers, one was a professor with French as L2, and Bill was an advanced-low speaker. Bill, who is not normally shy and is known to actively participate in conversations, tended to listen and not speak much. He made a conscious decision to let the natives dominate the situation, as they should have, in his opinion. There was no way he could keep up with the rapid-fire conversation, so he spoke only occasionally, showed interest with short phrases from his communicative repertoire, and did not acknowledge when the French was so fast that he could not make out what was said. This scenario contrasts with another dinner he attended where the native speakers tended to have slower rates of speech. Feeling much more comfortable and understanding almost all that was said, Bill participated actively. He also decided to let down his guard and fumbled on occasion, believing the native speakers would help construct the discourse he intended. Of the two scenarios, Bill felt the most comfortable in the second, and he eagerly accepted invitations to interact with those native speakers more than others.

Quick Reflection

In your classroom, do learners demonstrate agency? Do they try to speak in the L2? Do they try to use the L1? What speaker partners do they seek out in class? Do they seek you out? What is your reaction when learners exert their agency in your class?

What this example demonstrates is how one learner (in this case, one of the authors of this book) made decisions about who to interact with and how. He examined who he believed he could get the most out of in terms of learning experiences and sought them out more than others. In short, he made judgments about possible contexts of interaction and demonstrated his agency by choosing one type over another. In this way, he maximized his potential to continue acquiring French as opposed to abandoning it or waylaying it until some different context presented itself. Indeed, the fact that he accepted an opportunity to teach in Quebec that summer also demonstrates his agency. He wanted exposure to a French-speaking environment. In that case, he made a decision at the macro level of social factors, while his choices about who would be the best dinner partners was a micro-level decision.

Note that we can't say what Bill actually learned based on his exercising of agency. All we can say is that in so doing, he gave himself more affordances and contexts in which his French could continue to develop.

So, along with such things as disposition, social factors are important in terms of who learners interact with, how they interact, and that these factors in turn are implicated in how far learners get in learning and how their communication develops. Note that in terms of classrooms, social factors include whether a learner likes the class he or she is in, who the other classmates are and how they are viewed, what the learner thinks of the teacher, and so on. If you'd like to read more on social factors, we have listed some readings for you here:

Atkinson, D. (Ed.). (2011). *Alternative approaches to second language acquisition*. Routledge.

Duff, P. (2012). Identity, agency, and second language acquisition. In S. M. Gass & A. Mackey (Eds.), *The Routledge handbook of second language acquisition* (pp. 410–426). Routledge.

Véronique, G. D. (2013). Socialization. In J. Herschensohn & M. Young-Scholten (Eds.), *The Cambridge handbook of second language acquisition* (pp. 251–271). Cambridge University Press.

14. Don't different levels of learners need different things to help them keep learning?

Over the years, we've heard teachers make statements or ask questions such as the following: "Learners need a good foundation in the grammar early or they won't acquire language." "Isn't it the case that more advanced learners benefit from a different kind of instruction compared to beginners?" These statements are true if we buy into traditional curricula that are textbook based, and move from, say, beginning language to advanced courses in culture and literature. In such cases, curricula focus on the explicit learning of something (e.g., grammar, reading), not on the acquisition of language (or even communication). The ultimate goal is dictated by the demands of the content for language majors at the upper level. The same may happen with secondary students, where the demands of college-level programs dictate what they should "study" prior to entering college. In this FAQ, we won't speak to those needs. Instead, we will focus on language acquisition.

At every level of acquisition, input is needed, interaction is beneficial (possibly necessary), and the learning mechanisms a person brings to the task of language acquisition are the same. What does change is the quality of input and the quality of interaction. At the lowest levels or beginning phases, comprehensible communicatively embedded input is optimal when it involves short sentences, lots of repetition from the instructor, rephrasing of phrases, and so on. Here's an example in English, and we invite you to imagine the instructor speaking in the language you teach. (*Note:* This is Day 1 of class.)

> *The teacher holds up a picture of a dog. "This is a dog." The teacher holds up a picture of a cat. "This is a cat." Back to the dog. "This is a dog." Back to the cat. "This is a cat." Holding the picture of the dog. "Is this a dog or a cat? [Class shouts, "Dog!"] Yes. This is a dog." Holding the picture of the cat. "Is this a dog? [Class shouts, "No!"] No. This is a cat." The instructor tapes the pictures to the blackboard. Points to himself. "My name is Professor VanPatten." Points to a student. "Your name is Russ." Points to another student. "Your name is Terry."*

Points to the dog. "What is the dog's name? Is it Fido? [Class shrugs.] Is the dog's name Rover? [Again, shrugs and maybe a few shouts of "No."] Let's give the dog a name. The dog's name is Romeo. Class, what's the dog's name? [Class shouts "Romeo!"] Yes. The dog's name is Romeo." The instructor points to the cat. "Is this a dog? ["No!"] Is this a cat? ["Yes!"] Okay. This is a cat. The dog's name is Romeo. What's the cat's name? Is it Fluffy? [Shrugs, shouts of "No!"] Is it Tiger? [Shrugs, some responses of "maybe."] Let's give the cat a name. The dog's name is Romeo so let's call the cat …" The instructor speaks with rising intonation. [Class shouts, "Juliet!"] "Okay. Yes! The cat's name is Juliet and the dog's name is Romeo."

The teacher might follow up with short written texts that look something like this: "This is a dog. His name is Romeo. This is a cat. Her name is Juliet. Romeo loves Juliet. Juliet loves Romeo. But there's a problem …"

Now let's contrast this scenario with what might happen if this story and topic are introduced 6 months later by a teacher with a different group of learners (i.e., they were not part of the previous exchange, so the story is new to them).

The teacher puts up the two pictures on the blackboard. "Okay, class. Here are two animals. Which one is a dog? [Learners point.] And which one is a cat? [Learners point.] Great. So, we have a dog and a cat. Let's make a love story." The instructor draws a heart on the board. "A love story between a dog and a cat. But … does everyone know Shakespeare? [Learners nod or shout out "Yes!"] Name a love story from Shakespeare. ["Romeo and Juliet!"] Yes, Romeo and Juliet is a love story from Shakespeare. Okay. Let's call the dog Romeo and the cat Juliet. In Shakespeare, where do Romeo and Juliet meet? In a park, in a plaza, or at a party? ["At a party!"] Yes. They meet at a party. A masquerade party." The instructor mimics masquerade or a mask to indicate meaning. "But in the Shakespeare story, there is a problem. A really big problem. Two families are fighting. In our story, are there two families fighting? ["No!"] Who's fighting then? Two species are fighting." The teacher quickly provides a translation of species. "Romeo belongs to one species and Juliet belongs to another species. Can you think of some famous cartoons or movies where dogs and cats fight?" ["Tom and Jerry!" Class shouts out others.] And the class continues.

In the two scenarios, you can see that the roles of input and interaction with input don't change. What changes is the quality of the input, from shorter sentences to longer sentences and from many frequent pauses and comprehension checks to comprehension checks after a few sentences and not every sentence, for example. What also changes are the teacher's expectations about what the learners will or won't understand.

Now let's imagine learners in a class that is 2 years beyond the other class. The teacher is introducing the story for the first time. They are still in classes framed with input and interaction, but the quality of each has changed. Perhaps the teacher begins with a written text with missing information such as this:

> *"Years ago, there were two animals: Romeo, a dog, and Juliet, a cat. They came from species that fought. Dogs and cats did not get along. But one evening, at a party, ______________________________ . Later that night, Romero calls to Juliet from the garden. She is at her window. He is a dog, so he says ______________________________."*

And so on. The written input here is more complicated and more elaborate. It also shifts from relying on the immediacy of the present tense to shift narration into the past, and what the teacher will do is guide the class discussion to fill in the other parts of the story.

The point we're making is that it's not grammar and vocabulary or method that changes over time—it's the quality of input and interaction. Advanced learners need access to level-appropriate input just like beginners, and they need to interact with it just like beginners, and vice versa. What changes is how such things play out in classroom discourse and in the materials that teachers select and use.

Quick Reflection

Use the following prompt and imagine how you would help the class develop a story if they were a first-, second-, or third-year class: "Henry, a 13-year-old, is afraid of the dark." How does your input and interaction with learners change depending on level?

Let's touch on communication. Remember that communication is the expression and interpretation of meaning in a given context for a given purpose, and that when communication is problematic, interlocutors may enter into some kind of negotiation of meaning. In the early stages, learners clearly cannot express all the meaning they would like to communicate and they struggle to form full sentences. So, the first pass on communication is that learners move from focusing on interpretive abilities in communication with minimal free self-expression to increasing amounts of expressive ability, while interpretation is always present. At the same time, research suggests that there is an uneven relationship between learners and proficient or native speakers depending on the learners' level of ability. In the early stages of acquisition and well into the intermediate stage, learners are dependent on the other person for construction of discourse or interaction. That is, the other person takes the lead, helps scaffold the conversation, provides help to the learner should it be needed, and so on. The learner may be more reactive (i.e., less expressive) and unable to perform what we might consider routine communicative abilities (e.g., initiating or changing topics, asking questions). In terms of interaction, then, the learner progresses from complete dependence on the other person to moderate dependence to later becoming a full-fledged co-constructor of discourse and conversation.

These scenarios for communication, then, suggest that learners at different levels need different things from an instructor. In the earliest stages, learners need the instructor to lead the discourse, provide assistance, and overall manage how the conversation is constructed. The learner will need well-defined tasks that allow the learner to succeed in every sense of the term. In the intermediate stages, the learners will still need the instructor to play the same role, but perhaps a bit less so. At the advanced stages of acquisition, learners will not need such assistance from instructors except on rare occasions—but such interactions might look more like those between two proficient or native speakers of the language. Tasks might be less defined or, better yet, more open ended. For example, in the early stages, a task might have learners check boxes on a scale of one to five to indicate their reaction to particular statements, with the statements limited in number and the entire activity managed by the instructor. In the more advanced stages, a task might actually involve having learners make up the task themselves with more open parameters and less management from the instructor.

To be sure, the ideas presented in this FAQ are speculative to some extent while also being based on our experiences. There is no research we can direct you to that will indicate what is required or helpful at different levels. Ideas exist among veteran teachers who focus on acquisition and the development of communicative ability, and they would be a good source for additional ideas and concrete suggestions.

15. What is the best method for teaching language?

Over the years, we have heard from teachers who are concerned with methods—and rightly so. Many of them take courses called something like Methods of Language Teaching. For years, the profession had been dominated by the quest for "methods," to the point that things were never meant to be methods came to be called methods. For example, Communicative Language Teaching, which is an approach and overarching set of ideas, got co-opted by publishers and methods instructors, and now many teachers speak of the Communicative Method, when in reality there was never such a thing (and technically there still isn't). Recently, we have heard a few teachers talk about the Proficiency Method. These misuses of the term *method* are reflective of decades of a quest for the right method (e.g., the Direct Method, the Silent Way, Total Physical Response, the Audio-lingual Method, Teaching Proficiency through Reading and Storytelling). So, methods are on many teachers' minds in one way or another.

But maybe some readers aren't clear on what a method is. A method is a particular instantiation of procedure and technique derived from an approach. An approach, in turn, is a set of underlying beliefs about language learning. In theory, it is possible for an approach to spawn more than one method. Let's take a non-language example to start. If you want to build a gazebo, there are some underlying premises or beliefs. For example, the gazebo should be tall enough for most people to walk under. There must be some kind of roof. Something must support the roof. To be sure, there are other underlying premises. But note that two people can build gazebos in slightly different manners. One may include benches; another may not. One may use nails; another may use screws. One may use a slate roof, while another uses a tile roof. One may leave the wood raw and let it weather. Another may paint it. One may use wood as the flooring, and another may pour a concrete slab. The point is that out of basic ideas of what a gazebo is, different procedures and techniques may be employed to build one.

Languages aren't gazebos, of course, and it is difficult to imagine that more than one method emerges from basic ideas about acquisition. But it has happened. For example, from the basic idea that acquisition is input dependent (something that was a hypothesis in the 1960s but since the 1970s has become a fact; see Chapter 3), different methods have blossomed: Total Physical Response, the Natural Approach (which is really a method, not an approach), and Teaching Proficiency through Reading and Storytelling), among others.

Quick Reflection

What method informs your teaching, if any? Where do the ideas for this method come from? If you don't have a method, what determines what and how you teach?

At this juncture, we might ask why there have been successive waves of methods over the years. Why, with each generation, does a new method or a new way of teaching languages surface in the profession? In our opinion, this happens largely because such methods are looking to teach the same old thing but in a new way. That is, they assume that textbook vocabulary and textbook rules are what need to be learned, so they offer teachers new methods to do so. And for this reason, new methods fail to catch on. They are window dressing for "doing the same old thing." However, with research on language acquisition, it is questionable whether "methods" is a useful construct. In L2 research and theory, textbook rules, for example, are not assumed to make up mental representation. They are not what gets acquired in the end. For this reason, research on language acquisition is mute on how best to teach or what method to use. However, some of us—the authors of this book included—sometimes sit back and look at the totality of what we have come to know about how languages are acquired to fashion principles that might underlie language teaching. Taking this approach, we don't tell teachers how to teach. Instead, we offer principles and insights so that teachers can fashion their own methods. For example, in his book *While We're on the Topic*, Bill VanPatten outlines six principles that can inform contemporary language teaching. In another book, by H. Douglas Brown and Heekyeong Lee (*Teaching by Principles: An Interactive Approach to Language Pedagogy*), a similar tack is taken in which the concept of methods is eschewed in favor of insights from research and scholarship. This is not always what busy teachers want. A clear-cut method with a nice set of pre-fashioned materials suits teachers' hectic schedules much more than a handful of principles from which they must figure out on their own just what to do and how to do it.

However, offering principles and insights from research is the honest way of talking with language teachers, and it is the only way to honestly answer the question "Which method is best?" ACTFL, for example, has taken a similar approach to the issue in its publication and advocacy of "high-leverage teaching practices." Although we don't agree with some of these practices, and we question their origin in both research and theory about languages and language acquisition, we acknowledge that using guidelines and principles is the way to go. We need to empower teachers to create for themselves and to share ideas with each other. Like politics, language teaching is local. And language classrooms might look different in places such as Sacramento, Atlanta, and rural Pennsylvania.

When it comes to language acquisition, as described in this book, let's look at three possible conclusions a teacher might make. The first is this. Given that instruction in grammar has little effect on how the mental representation of language evolves over time in the learner's mind, the teacher might ask herself, "Why bother with teaching grammar? Explicit teaching and practice are not how language actually gets in my students' heads." That would be a reasonable position based on what we know about acquisition. But there are other possibilities. Another teacher might say that, given that classroom learners build linguistic systems in their heads independently of instruction, instruction doesn't really hurt, so why not just keep doing what we're doing with grammar and vocabulary? Learners will eventually get language anyway. And a third teacher might arrive at some middle area in which instruction in grammar isn't thrown out but is minimized in some way or makes up but a fraction of what happens in the curriculum.

That said, we need to keep in mind that knowledge about acquisition is only one factor that informs teachers' decision-making. We mentioned some of those factors in our prologue. Let's imagine the first teacher described, who says, "Okay. Teaching grammar isn't important. Let's get rid of it." Can that teacher do that with the curriculum she is handed? What kind of autonomy does she have? Does she have to coordinate with other teachers? How will she assign grades in a system that is dependent on student GPAs and "progress reports"? What materials does she have at her disposal? Because of such factors, research from acquisition alone cannot fashion a method or curriculum for teachers. We reiterate what we said earlier: Like politics, language teaching is local. So, language classrooms might look different in places such as Sacramento, Atlanta, and rural Pennsylvania.

If there is one principle or insight for the classroom that emerges from acquisition research, it is this: The more that learners have access to communicatively embedded input, the richer the opportunities for growth of the linguistic system in their heads. Without such input, acquisition of language is hampered. But we should note that acquisition research does not tell teachers how to get more input into the classroom. As we noted, various methods have emerged based on this one insight. There is no one way to get as much communicatively embedded input into the classroom as possible. And we certainly cannot tell teachers what kinds of topics and themes are interesting to them and their students. What is more, the research shows that learners must be actively engaged with such input. That is, there must be some kind of interaction that heightens learners' attention and their involvement and interest. For teachers who'd like to explore this topic and how it plays out in the classroom, we suggest Bill's book *While We're on the Topic,* also published by ACTFL. (See especially Principle 4 and the epilogue.)

There is no research on the topic of best methods that we can recommend, or at least no current research. Research on particular methods died out by the 1980s. Most current research related to classrooms is not centered on particular methods, but instead on whether or not to explicitly teach grammar and vocabulary. (See Chapter 4 for a discussion of that issue.) Even ACTFL does not prescribe particular methods. Maybe it's best to forget about a "best" method and to think instead about outcomes and how we can get there. And keep in mind what we said in the prologue: The best decisions teachers can make are informed decisions. Having knowledge about language acquisition is part of being informed.

Here are two sources cited in this FAQ:

Brown, D., & Lee, H. (2015). *Teaching by principles: An interactive approach to language pedagogy* (4th ed.). Pearson Educational.

VanPatten, B. (2017). *While we're on the topic.* ACTFL.